ON BEING HUMAN

ON BEING HUMAN

Principles of Ethics

Andrew C. Varga, S.J.

PAULIST PRESS
New York, N.Y./Ramsey, N.J.

Library of Congress
Catalog Card Number: 78-51589

ISBN: 0-8091-2111-5

Published by Paulist Press
Editorial Office: 1865 Broadway, New York, N.Y. 10023
Business Office: 545 Island Road, Ramsey, N.J. 07446

Printed and bound in the
United States of America

Contents

Preface

As many books on ethics are published every year, a new work in this field needs some justification.

Having used various textbooks in the teaching of ethics, I have encountered the problem of giving my students, a concise textbook that presents the fundamental ethical questions in a coherent and systematic manner. Most textbooks, however, give a survey of the various ethical systems and leave it to the student to develop and validate his own ethical theory. This method is usually followed for the laudable purpose of avoiding indoctrination and undue pressure on the intellectual freedom of the student. But in my experience, the task of building a well structured ethical system is too difficult, if not entirely impossible, for the beginner. An attempt is made, therefore, in this book to present the major ethical questions in a structured and consistent way. At the same time, the student is left free to accept or reject certain principles by weighing the arguments pro and con.

This book, nevertheless, does not intend to promote the idea of a shallow and relativistic pluralism which holds that it does not matter what ethical principles we follow in our conduct as long as we are consistent. Rather it is argued that there is a difference between right and wrong, that not all principles are correct and that it matters a great deal what ethical system we accept for our private and public affairs. A definite stand is taken for the existence of objective morality and for a natural law approach in building a valid ethical system. The main objective of the book is to show that morality is based on human nature. The detailed study of human nature, however, is left to the discipline called Philosophy of Man.

The book is meant not only for the college student but also for any person who wants some philosophical and common sense guidance concerning the morality of the decisions he has to make every day.

This work does not propose an original ethical system. Its purpose is to present the wisdom of great moralists systematically and in a language that can be understood by educated persons of our times. If there is anything new in it, it is the method of presentation rather than the content. It has clearly been influenced by many moralists of the natural law tradition, the influence being sometimes more in the form of integrated knowledge as a result of readings and studies rather than traceable to one or another particular author.

I owe gratitude to many persons who helped me in this work, especially to my colleagues at four different institutions with whom I had fruitful exchanges of ideas. I am grateful to my colleagues and friends who read the first draft of the manuscript and gave encouragement and useful suggestions for its improvement. I want to thank especially Dr. Bernard B. Gilligan, of Fordham University, who read and corrected the final draft; and Rev. John A. Adam, S.J., who read the manuscript carefully and gave helpful criticism and welcome encouragement. Needless to say, all the shortcomings are mine.

I
The Subject Matter of Ethics

Anthropologists and historians have gathered many data which indicate that the problem of good and evil is as old as the human race. Elaborate codes of conduct existed in ancient times prescribing the right way of action and forbidding the evil. In most pristine cultures the religious and civil spheres were not as clearly separated as they are in our times; the state tried to educate its subjects to be good persons from both the religious and civic points of view, which actually were considered as one. Being a good citizen meant observing the laws of God or the gods. A good Jew, for instance, had to observe the laws of Yahweh.

Ancient thinkers and legislators most probably reflected on the nature of *the good*, on the factors that make an act good or bad, and particularly on the question of what is good for man. Ethics, then, did not begin with modern, or even with ancient Greek, philosophy. Nevertheless, the term itself was first used in Greece and the systematic philosophical study of good and evil is customarily attributed to Greek philosophers. Even the English term, ethics, is derived from the study developed by the Greeks.

The root of the term, *ethics*, is *ethos*, a Greek word which means custom. Early Greek philosophers

1

observed that some customs are more stable and unchangeable than others, and they undertook the task of examining the difference between changing customs (the ways of dressing, fashion, different methods of preparing food by various ethnic groups, etc.) and stable customs (keeping promises, telling the truth, respecting the property and life of others, etc.). They called the study of the stable ways of conduct *Ethika*. Hence we have the English term, "ethics."

Ethics investigates the reasons why certain actions are universally considered good or bad, prescribed or forbidden. It seeks to give an answer to the question of whether there is something in the nature of an act that determines its rightness or wrongness, or whether, on the contrary, the quality of rightness or wrongness is attached to an act from without.

Ancient Roman philosophers, generally following the opinion of the classical Greek philosophers, translated the Greek terminology of ethics into Latin. The plural form of the Latin word for "ethos" (custom) is "mores." Hence ethics was called "philosophia moralis" in Latin, and the English words of "moral" and "morality" are derivations of the Latin words, "moralis" and "moralitas."

Ethics can be defined as the study of the rightness and wrongness of human actions.

Positive and Normative Sciences

In order to understand the nature of the study of morality, we have to see to which class of sciences ethics belongs. According to well established tradition, sciences are either positive or normative.

Positive or descriptive sciences describe objects and phenomena but do not pass judgment on their subject matter. They are not concerned with questions of good and evil. Physics, chemistry and biology are examples of positive sciences.

Normative sciences, on the other hand, deal with rules, norms or criteria by which the objects of their inquiry are judged. Normative sciences prescribe rules of judgment or action; they are prescriptive.

Aesthetics, for example, deals with norms according to which we judge the objects of perception to be beautiful or ugly.

Logic establishes the criteria by which we judge whether our reasoning is valid or not.

Ethics belongs to the class of normative sciences because it examines and validates the standards by which we judge our actions to be right or wrong, good or evil.

The normative sciences are concerned not only with the practical application of norms and rules but also with the fundamental question of whether the norms are valid and of how their validity can be established.

In recent literature, the study of the validity of ethical norms is called *metaethics*.

II
The Good in General

In order to understand what is meant by the goodness or badness of human actions, it will be useful to examine the usage of the term *good*.

First of all, we have to see what, in general, terms or words stand for. They are symbols and stand for something; they represent some reality. The human mind turns toward the world around us and, exploring this reality, comes to know many objects. As we communicate with each other we use words or symbols for the objects we know. The vocabulary of a child or an adult grows with the growth of his knowledge of reality.

Some of the objects around us can easily be identified—for instance, a house, an apple, a brick. We can easily define or describe the meaning of these words. There are some things, however, which cannot be easily identified or described—for instance, the realities for which the terms "faithful," "just," "beautiful," "good" stand. Nevertheless, we use these terms frequently and we definitely mean something by them. What is the reality behind these words? Do we all mean the same thing or do we imply different forms of reality? It seems that, notwithstanding the fact that we cannot easily define these terms, some common elements are attributed by everybody to the reality for which these terms stand.

We mean something by these words, and a studious analysis can reveal the reality beyond the words. "Good" is perhaps one of the most frequently used terms in our language and since the goodness or badness of human acts is the subject matter of our study, we have to undertake the analysis of this term in order to understand its meaning. It will be useful in the process of this search to try to find the most general meaning of the term "good" and then investigate later what good means in reference to human actions.

Two Different Ways of Using the Term "Good"

1. We use the attribute "good" in reference to many things. We state that a certain car is good; we speak of good weather, good food, etc. A farmer may say that the rain was good. Yet persons who wanted to go on a picnic affirm that the rain was bad. If you want to go skiing, you will hold a big snowfall good. Those who have to drive a car in snow, will call it bad.

It seems, then, that we frequently use the term, good, in a *relative* way. We refer an action, an object or a happening to some natural or freely chosen goal and call it good or bad according to its contribution toward reaching that goal. The farmer will state that the rain is good because it helps his crops to grow. It contributes to achieving the fullness, the totality, of his wheat or corn. Too much rain would be bad because it would make the crop rot. What determines the right amount of rain, the "goodness" of rain, in reference to the crop? It seems that it is determined by the nature of that particular crop. For instance wheat needs less water, less rain, than rice.

This short analysis of the common usage of the term, good, leads us to the conclusion that the goodness of an object or event is sometimes derived from a natural goal. All beings have a nature, and certain actions or objects are compatible with this nature, helping it in its growth or the completion of its being, to reach the full potential of this nature. Other actions or objects are incompatible with a certain nature and consequently harm it, stunt it. We call these objects or actions, "bad."

Sometimes the goal we pursue is not a natural one, but one we freely chose for ourselves. For instance, we decide to go skiing or sailing. Abundant snow or sufficient wind, which help us to reach these goals, are considered good; facts which prevent us from realizing our goals, as above-freezing temperature or heavy storm, are called bad.

We also design things such as machines, houses, bridges, etc., and the necessary parts or actions, the carburetor for a car, the skill of the mason, which fit into the design, are termed good; parts and actions which do not contribute to the realization of the design are rejected and are called bad.

The previous analysis revealed that certain actions or things are called good because they are *instruments* for the achievement of a nature or a freely chosen goal. The reality of the connection of the action or object with the goal is called good. In this sense, we use the term *good* relatively and not absolutely, because we consider the goodness of the event or object in reference to something else, and not in itself.

2. We use the term "good," however, also in an unrelated way, that is, we consider certain objects in themselves, without further reference, and call them good. A crop that has grown to its full potential is called a good crop. An apple tree that bears plenty of

fine apples is called a good apple tree without further reference to the possible income a farmer can get by selling the apples. When a being achieves the fullness of its potential, the totality of its being, it is termed good. In other words, the reality of completeness according to the nature or design of a thing is the quality that makes a thing good. A being that has achieved its full potential is sometimes called perfect, which is another word for completeness. "Perfect" comes from the Latin word "perfectus," which means "made whole, made complete."

As a conclusion, we can state that the previous analysis indicates that the term "good" is used either in a relative or an absolute way, that is, an object or action can be referred to some goal and called good in reference to that goal, or a thing can be considered in itself and termed good because of its completeness.

III
The Moral Good

After having analyzed the general meaning of the term *good*, we can examine the specific application of this concept to human beings since the subject matter of our study is the good or evil that is found in man.

Good has different meanings as we use this word in connection with men. We can state of a person that he is a good sportsman, a good cook, a good surgeon etc., or we can simply state that he is a good man. When we are asked whether a famous sportsman is a good man, we understand that there is a difference between being a good sportsman and a good man. A good sportsman or a good surgeon can be good human beings, but they are not good men by virtue of their eminence in sports or skill in surgery. We understand that something more is demanded to be called simply a good man without further qualification. When we state that a person is good, we mean that he is a good human being. He is good in his humanity and not just in one or another skill of human nature. This specific human goodness is called *the moral good*.

What makes a person morally good? A person is not born morally good or bad. He becomes good or bad by performing good or bad actions as he grows up. Consequently, if we want to get to the source of human goodness—in other words, to the constitutive factor of the moral good, we have to analyze the human act and find the quality or property that makes it good.

How can we determine the rightness or wrongness of human actions? Our previous examination of the general meaning of the term good will help us in this task for we have to use the same procedure here in our search for the moral good as we did in our pursuit of the general meaning of good. Certain actions such as truthfulness, keeping promises, fulfilling one's duties, are universally called good because they are related to the idea of a perfect human nature since these actions build the true humanity in a person. There is some quality in these actions which contributes to the completion, the perfection of man, so that we can speak of a true human being and not of somebody who is "inhuman" in his actions. But what is the completeness, the fullness, the perfection of man?

It seems that we have to give some answer to this question lest we go in circles. Somehow "the man in the street" or the educated person has an idea of what human beings are or should be. Individuals who deviate from their idea of man are considered evil because such individuals are stunted in their humanity.

The various ethical systems developed from ancient times up to our present era, propose different ideas of the fulfillment or completion of man in his humanity. These different ideas basically reflect their understanding or theory of what man is. If man is principally just a sense being, then any action which produces sense pleasure becomes morally good because it completes and fulfills man in his humanity. If man is considered principally a rational and social being, then actions that promote rational conduct and harmonious living with one's fellow men are the morally good acts because they build the truly human in us. The goodness or badness of an action is determined by its relationship to the idea of true humanness.

Ethical systems differ from one another by proposing different ideas of what it means to be human. An authentic philosophy of man is consequently an important and necessary element for the understanding of the principles of morality.

The particular way certain philosophers consider man sets the *standard* or *norm* by which the rightness or wrongness of an action is determined. A *norm, standard*, or *criterion of morality* in this sense, then, means a measure which can be compared with the human act, thus revealing the goodness or badness of the act. We are familiar with the various standards of measure in everyday use. We use different measures of length, weight, volume, temperature, etc. Although there may be some connection between a measure and some natural fact (for instance, the length of a "foot"), we are aware that measures as we use them today are based on conventions. There are international agreements concerning the metric or the Anglo-Saxon measures, and the Bureau of Standards in the U.S. assures the uniform compliance with the accepted standards.

The question of whether the standard or measure of morality is based on convention or on some natural fact is essential for the moral life of mankind and touches the central problem of morality. The answer to this question reflects one's idea of what kind of a being man is. To help our search for the authentic norm of morality, we will examine the major ethical systems as they explain their understanding of what the morally good act is. We will point out their strong points and their weak points, so that we may develop our own discernment of morality and then describe and validate the norm which reveals to us the rightness or wrongness of human actions.

IV
The Human Act

Before undertaking the scrutiny of the various ethical systems, we have to determine where exactly we have to look for the moral good or moral evil. Men are not born morally good or bad but become good or bad by performing good or bad actions as they develop and grow up. It seems, then, that goodness or badness is located in some way in the human act. It follows from this observation that the understanding of the structure and nature of the human act is essential in our search for morality. Philosophical psychology deals with this matter; here we simply summarize its findings. For a detailed study of this question we should turn to psychology or the philosophy of man.

Man differs from animals especially by his faculties of intellect and free will. Some actions we perform do not differ in their character from the actions of animals because they are not under the influence of the intellect and free will. For instance, although they are performed by man, reflex actions or actions performed while the person is completely distracted are not specifically human acts because the intellect and free will are not the causes of their existence.

Man performs many acts which apparently have the same characteristics as those performed by animals. Eating, hearing, seeing, running away from pain or seeking pleasure, all seem to be the same acts in human beings as in animals. The human act, however, differs from that of the animals by the knowledge of the act and the freedom to perform it. While animals have some knowledge and consciousness (which principally is sense knowledge and some vague consciousness differing from the self-consciousness of man) their actions are prompted and determined by instincts and desires. A hungry animal cannot abstain from eating the food that is given it unless a stronger desire (to avoid pain, a beating, etc.) checks the desire to eat it. Animals are trained and conditioned by reward and punishment, by pleasure and pain, but they do not really learn intellectually.

The specifically human act, then, is one of which man is conscious and which is freely performed. There is no really human act without knowledge of the object of the act, because to be human means to be governed by the intellect. Knowledge is essential also for the exercise of freedom because there cannot be a truly free choice without the knowledge of the object of our will. The will is blind without the information gained by the intellect. When we act in a human way, first we apprehend the object of our act and then we freely proceed to perform it.

Knowledge and freedom give us mastery over the act. The act is truly ours and we are responsible for it. *Responsibility* proceeds from knowledge and freedom.

Since morality, as the specifically human good, resides in the truly human act, it follows that freedom of choice and the resulting responsibility are the prerequisites of morality.

V
Free Will and Determinism

It is logical to state that there is no responsibility without freedom of choice. But is it self-evident that man has the ability freely to choose among alternative courses of action? The doctrine of determinism affirms that, in spite of all appearances, man is not free in his actions.

Before we review the arguments for freedom and determinism, the concepts of freedom and determinism have to be clarified to avoid misunderstandings.

Free Will

The principle of causality affirms that no effect or action can be produced without an adequate cause; there are no causeless phenomena. Freedom of choice does not mean that free acts have no causes, but rather that the will, as the cause of an act, has the ability to determine itself, since it is capable of causing different courses of action or is capable of abstaining from an action under certain circumstances.[1]

Freedom in general is the absence of coercion. This is, however, only a negative aspect of freedom (freedom *from*); its positive aspect (freedom *for*) always expresses a surge of energy toward reaching a goal, performing the act intended.

Coercion may be physical, psychological or

moral. The absence of *physical coercion* is called *freedom of spontaneity*. A dog is "free" to run around when it is untied. When a criminal is condemned to a prison term, we say that he has lost his freedom, meaning freedom of spontaneity, because he cannot move around freely, cannot leave the jail.

The absence of *psychological* or *intrinsic coercion* is called *psychological freedom* or *freedom of choice*. This is the essence of free will as it is commonly understood. This freedom is the basis and source of responsibility since the free act belongs to the person who performed it and could have abstained from it. It is claimed that animals do not have this intrinsic psychological freedom because they are compelled by their instincts and drives to perform certain actions. A hungry dog is forced by his desire to satisfy his hunger to eat the available food. A hungry man, however, can refuse to eat; he can even go on a hunger strike and starve himself to death.

Absence of intrinsic coercion is the negative aspect of freedom. Its positive characteristic could be described as the ability of the will to act or not act and to act in various ways when all conditions for acting are present. The ability to abstain from an act or perform an act is called *freedom of exercise*. Thus, deliberately abstaining from an act is a free choice and it can be imputed to us. In every day language we call this an act of omission. It is evident that we are responsible for deliberate omissions when we could have performed an act and were obliged to perform it. A person is responsible, for instance, for not paying his taxes or not writing his term paper.

When we decide to act, we frequently have several alternatives. Planning to spend the afternoon by relaxing, one can go to the movies, play ball, listen to music, etc. The ability to choose among these alternatives is called freedom of specification.

In addition to the previous forms of coercion, we can speak of *moral coercion*. A law that obliges the tourist to pay certain custom duties on articles bought abroad does not remove his ability to choose to hide the articles and avoid paying the duty. He is, however, not "free" to do it; that is, he is not free *morally*. If the law restricting the import of certain articles is repealed, the tourist becomes "free" to bring in those objects. This type of freedom means the absence of moral coercion, and it is called *moral freedom* or *freedom of independence* to distinguish it from psychological freedom. A colony becomes "free" when it gains independence from the laws of the mother country.

When we speak of *social and political freedom*, we usually mean the absence of undue pressures of social circumstances, like class or race distinctions or the tyrannical rule of one political party or one group of people. This freedom should not be confused with freedom of choice in the philosophical sense of the term.

Determinism

The precondition of responsibility and morality is freedom of choice or psychological freedom. Determinism denies the existence of this kind of freedom and holds that, in spite of all appearances, we are not free in our actions but are compelled by various factors to act only in one specific way.

Biological determinism holds that heredity, the kind of body we have, with all its physiological interactions and biological laws, determines all our actions.

How we behave depends on our biological make-up.

Many behaviorists, especially B. F. Skinner, argue that the environment determines our conduct. The character and behavior of a person are entirely the product of the social and physical milieu. Responsibility and morality, then, have no meaning in this theory. Nobody should be punished for his deeds but only put in a better milieu, one that would change his behavior.

> It is in the nature of an experimental analysis of human behavior that it should strip away the functions previously assigned to autonomous man and transfer them one by one to the controlling environment . . .[2]

According to this theory man can be manipulated by his environment and his behavior is the sum total of the effects of his milieu.

Sigmund Freud proposed the theory that the *unconscious* has a determining role in our actions and freedom of choice is only an appearance. Psychoanalysis can shed light on the hidden causes of our actions.

Psychological determinism affirms that the strongest motive is the determining cause of our actions. Man simply reviews the motives and the recognition of the strongest motive settles the course of action. Motive sometimes is understood to be the desire of the person and thus the strongest desire would govern the actions of man.

Theological determinism is the doctrine that God has predetermined the course of the universe, including the activities of men, at least to the extent that the eternal destiny of man is fixed. This doctrine is called predestination. God is sometimes identified with Fate and the theory becomes quite vague since no clear definition of the nature of Fate is given and it is not explained who or what is responsible for the operation of Fate. The belief in Fate leads to fatalism, to the persuasion that all events take place by the force of Fate and human beings cannot alter the course of events.

Some form of theological determinism sometimes appears in the conviction of God-fearing persons who attribute all accidents to the "will of God" and not so much to the carelessness or negligence of freely operating human beings.

The Existence of Freedom of Choice

Believers in freedom of choice do not affirm that all our actions are free. They admit that the influence of environment, physiological malfunctioning of the nervous system, certain inherited traits, certain psychological forces as in cases of kleptomania or pyromania, psychoses or neuroses, may become so powerful that a person can lose his freedom of action. They affirm, nevertheless, that men in general are free in many of their actions and are responsible for what they deliberately and knowingly do.

The following reasons are usually offered for the existence of freedom of choice.

1. *Immediate awareness of freedom.* Philosophical psychology emphasizes the fact that all men have a direct consciousness of free decisions. We assume this freedom before the act and are conscious of our freedom in the performance of the act. We know that we have the ability to choose between alternative courses of action. Direct and internal experience means that

we have a firsthand knowledge of the fact of freedom. Nothing is closer to us and more transparent to the scrutiny of our intellect than the experience of a free choice, in which we are so intimately involved. We can reflect upon our free decision while we make the decision, and the immediate experience of this freedom gives us a reassurance that our knowledge is not mistaken.

2. *Indirect awareness of freedom.* This awareness is revealed in the fact of deliberation before the act. We weigh the arguments pro and con because we know that it is ultimately up to us to come to a decision one way or the other.

3. *Conviction of personal responsibility.* All mature persons accept responsibility for actions they freely and deliberately perform. As children grow and their ability to choose freely also grows, their sense of responsibility also appears.

As we accept responsibility for our own actions, similarly we hold others responsible for their deeds. Life in society is based on this sense of responsibility, without which no orderly human community would be possible.

4. *Consensus of the existence of freedom.* There is a consensus that human beings are free. This consensus is revealed by many facts in society. As we accept our own responsibility for our own actions, so we judge others. We become indignant, for example, when we are robbed or mugged. Even persons who are professional determinists act as if they were free and participate in this general consensus by their expressions, ways of acting, planning, etc. Even psychiatrists who accept Freudian determinism, act as if men were free because they try to restore some degree of free-

dom of choice to those patients who are beset by compulsive actions.

One could object that even the most general consensus of the whole human race could be mistaken. Mankind universally believed for a long time, for instance, that the sun revolved around the earth. The fact of freedom of choice, however, is a different form of consciousness. It is based on an internal and personal direct experience and knowledge; it is not a scientific phenomenon distinct from us and which cannot be directly experienced.

5. *Administration of justice.* Our society is based on the conviction that men are responsible for their actions because they have freedom of choice. Civilized nations have a system whereby they first examine the degree of freedom of an accused person. If he is found mentally deranged, even if his insanity was only temporary, he is not held responsible for an offense, and instead of punishment, some form of treatment is prescribed to restore his freedom if it is possible. In most cases, however, the fact of freedom and responsibility is easily proved and the administration of justice is based on this fact.

6. Social environment and cultural background certainly do influence our preferences and choices, but this pressure of the environment rarely amounts to such a force as to compel our actions. The fact that many persons change their opinions including ingrained prejudices as they mature and reflect upon their life, indicates that the environment does not deprive us of our freedom.

7. It is evident that we cannot perform a really human act without a knowledge of the goal of the action or without having a motive for it. Psychological

determinism affirms that we are just impartial analyzers of the weight of motives and that we necessarily follow the strongest motive. But what is the strongest motive? The answer given is similar to the Darwinian maxim of the survival of the fittest. By definition, the fittest is the one that survived. This is tautology, however, and does not really answer the question. Similarly, the answer that the strongest motive is the one that wins, does not escape being a tautology. What really happens is that we can make one of the motives be the winner. Experience tells us that sometimes we choose only an apparent good against our "better judgment" and we know that "stronger" arguments militate for the opposite action. The will is not forced by the motive, but the person freely decides to follow one or the other motive.

Freedom of choice does not primarily consist in trivial decisions, such as choosing steak rather than fried chicken on the menu. Freedom of choice is especially revealed in decisions where moral values are involved. For instance: Should I procure an abortion or not? Should I steal this book from the university book store or not? Should I volunteer to work in a hospital ten hours a week or spend this time watching television?

Human freedom is especially exercised in an act of commitment to worthy goals, for instance, choosing a vocation or profession in life. Commitment to a goal effects the whole life of a person and influences him to direct many of his daily activities to the end he has chosen. A college student may decide to become a physician. This decision will naturally direct many of his activities toward his goal. He will have to choose the proper premedical subjects in college, must study hard to get into a medical school, etc. When he gets his medical degree, his original decision to become a physician continues to influence his whole life-style. One should not call his actions determined, however, because they are only the execution of his free decision made many years before. The free choice is lived out and carried out in detail in one's life. It is the logic of action that the person who wants an end must also choose the means. There are, of course, less momentous decisions in life than choosing a vocation, but human freedom is especially exercised also in less weighty decisions when values are involved. In ethics we consider specifically these free decisions as the proper subject of morality.

The argument from the immediate awareness of freedom is called into question by some determinists who point out that a person may be hypnotized to carry out certain orders after awakening from the hypnotic trance. For instance, a person may be ordered to go to the door and open it. As he carries out this order, he is allegedly aware of a free choice of opening the door, and yet his action is determined by the previous hypnosis. On the other hand, it is a fact that persons cannot be ordered in hypnosis to perform actions which are against their value convictions or commitments. This again indicates that human freedom is particularly exercised in the choice of values and commitments to worthy goals and that our immediate awareness of freedom in these cases remains a valid insight into the function and existence of free will.

Levels of Freedom and Responsibility

The subject matter of ethics is the free, and consequently responsible, human act. The previous paragraphs dealt with this subject and surveyed the reasons supporting the existence of freedom of choice. The question can be asked, however, whether all free acts are equally free or whether there may not be different levels of freedom and consequently different degrees of responsibility. The answer to this question evidently has great importance for personal morality and the administration of justice.

Every free act must be the result of a knowledge of the object of the act and of the ability of the will to choose, i.e., both intellect and will contribute to a free act. Both faculties, however, can be affected in their functioning by certain factors which may alter a person's degree of freedom and responsibility. Psychology deals extensively with the factors that inhibit our knowledge and the functioning of the will. For our purpose, it will suffice to list some of these influences and to comment on them from the ethical point of view.

Influences Affecting the Intellect

Attention and distraction can be present in various degrees. Everybody can ascertain this by reflecting upon his own consciousness. We have a duty to "pay attention" to what we are doing, especially when the act is important. Popular courses of "mind-control" techniques propose exercises to increase our power of concentration. Nevertheless, it may happen that a person is inculpably distracted and does not pay enough attention to what he is doing. Distraction limits our clear knowledge of the object of an act and it may diminish responsibility. Not every distraction, however, will remove responsibility. A driver, for instance, must pay attention to the road and traffic, and when he realizes that he cannot concentrate because of tiredness or other impediments, he must stop driving.

Ignorance similarly affects the rational part of a free act. Ignorance that cannot be overcome is called *invincible* ignorance in technical language. This occurs if we don't even suspect that we are in the state of ignorance concerning certain aspects of a voluntary act. Thus a mailman may not surmise that there is a bomb in the package he delivers. Ignorance sometimes cannot be overcome even after diligent investigation because some aspects of the act are not understood by us.

In other cases ignorance can be overcome by a simple investigation or inquiry. This type of ignorance is called *vincible*.

Upon reflection of the consequences of ignorance we can conclude that invincible ignorance removes responsibility; vincible ignorance, on the other hand, does not remove responsibility, but it may lessen culpability.

Prejudice is an ingrained way of forming opinions without sufficient ground about the characteristics of certain persons, races, religions, etc. When a person discovers or suspects that his actions are guided by prejudices, he has the duty to remedy his ignorance. Otherwise, he will be morally responsible for any injury caused to others.

Ignorance may refer to the consequences of an action. One may inculpably fail to *foresee* the consequences of a free act and thus responsibility may be diminished or, in some cases, may be entirely removed. One has the duty, however, to consider the consequences of a free act and avoid possible damage to others.

Fear is a word that can have different meanings. It may mean the awareness or anticipation of some danger or unpleasant event, or it may signify a strong emotion of trepidation and anxiety because of the threat of something unpleasant. Fear in the first sense affects the intellect, while in the second sense it may also affect the will. A student is afraid of failing a course if he does not write his term paper. This fear will motivate him to go to the library and begin the research for his paper. This is an example of fear in the first sense. A foreign agent tells you that he has embarrassing information about you, which he will reveal unless you consent to turn over secret data to him, data to which you have access as a government employee. This is another example of fear in the first sense.

Does fear, understood in the first sense, remove responsibility? Is any action motivated by fear an irrational or forced action? The fear of failure motivates the student to work hard and we certainly do not want to deprive him of the merit of his hard work. He did work deliberately and consciously. Does the fear of embarrassment justify telling lies? Are the civil servant or the soldier excused for spying or betraying their country because of the threat of pain or embarrassment? It seems that fear, understood in the first sense, does not remove responsibility because the person is still in the possession of his faculties and he can decide to cooperate or refuse cooperation with the enemy.

Fear, however, may be increased to such an extent that it becomes duress, intimidation, psychological torture or brainwashing. In these cases it affects not only the intellect but also the will and may destroy freedom and responsibility.

Factors Affecting the Will

Man naturally desires pleasure and tries to avoid pain or unpleasant feelings. *Passion* is understood as a strong motion of the sense appetite reaching out for pleasure or running away from pain. The glutton, who constantly overeats and cannot resist the pleasure of eating, succumbs to passion.

Passion that is deliberately aroused is called consequent passion. One may brood over an insult and can be aroused to such a degree by the desire for revenge that he cannot control himself when he meets his enemy.

Passion that arises spontaneously, before one can rationally control oneself, is called antecedent passion, as it precedes the awareness of the intellect and the deliberate control of the will. Some persons may easily lose their "temper," as a "quick-tempered" person may when we step on his toes.

Growing up means, among other things, to learn to control ourselves. Nevertheless, antecedent passion may sometimes remove responsibility, or lessen it. Consequent passion, on the other hand, is a deliberate and voluntary act.

Torture, both psychological and physical, may become so intense that the desire to get rid of the pain can break a person's will and remove responsibility for an act. It is known that totalitarian regimes have developed sophisticated methods of physical and psychological torture that even the strongest person cannot resist. Nobody can really judge how long a person can withstand torture, but it is clear that at a certain point the will may lose control. The desire to stop the torture and pressure may become so overwhelming that freedom and responsibility are removed.

Force is physical compulsion, and when it happens against a person's consent, it removes responsibility.

Habit is a behavior pattern acquired by the repetition of the same act or by the use of certain drugs, facilitating the performance of certain actions. In order to lead a normal human life, we have to acquire many habits, such as writing, reading, speaking, walking, driving a car, playing musical instruments, typing, etc. In another direction, it is well known that certain drugs, such as tobacco, alcohol, heroin, etc., are habit-forming and may create physiological dependence.

We are not responsible for unintentionally acquired habits, e.g., swearing learned in childhood, but we are obliged to overcome the habit when we discover it and learn that it is morally disordered or harmful.

One is responsible for intentionally acquired habits and for actions resulting from these habits. An alcoholic or a drug addict, for instance, who deliberately or at least knowingly developed the habit in spite of warnings of friends and parents is responsible for his addiction and for acts performed by the force of his habit, since he foresaw the consequences. The cause that produced the results was voluntary and consequently the effects are also voluntary. We call these effects *voluntary in cause.*

Psychology and psychiatry examine many other factors that can diminish freedom of the will. Neurosis and psychosis impede the free self-determination of the will. It is difficult to say at what point a person becomes abnormal and not responsible for his action, but it is evident from cases of abnormality that freedom can be lost. Even the weather can influence a person's reactions, moods and alertness so that his responsibility can thereby be affected.

VI
Is Morality Made
or Discovered?

As we have previously observed, man becomes morally good or bad by performing good or bad actions. Morality, then, has to be looked for in the human act. In order to facilitate this investigation, we have analyzed the structure and basic characteristics of the human act. We are ready now to begin our search for the factor that makes a human act good or bad. In order to avoid misunderstandings, we have to note that a human act is not simply some physical action as, for instance, the rescue of a person who is drowning. The human act is primarily the act of the will that is directed to the object. Nevertheless, the will is not complete unless it is carried out or, at least, there is a serious attempt to carry out the decision. The will to rescue a drowning person, for example, is completed by making a serious attempt to save him.

The chemist can analyze a substance in his laboratory and find the characteristic actions and reactions of that object within that same object. He does not make the laws himself and does not attach them to that particular being, but discovers the laws within the object. An atomic physicist does not make the laws of atomic energy but discovers them in the atom.

Can we state something similar of the human act?

Is the factor that makes it good or bad found within the act itself or is it added to it from without? Is morality intrinsic or extrinsic, objective or subjective?

If the factor that makes the act good or bad is added from without, who adds this element to the act? Is it the individual who acts? Is he arbitrarily free to declare what actions he considers good or bad so that good and bad become subjective and relative concepts as they depend on the changing moods or whims of the acting person? Is the person limited by some objective facts even if they are extrinsic to the act, so that morality would be more stable and objective? Is it society or public authority that determines the rightness or wrongness of an act? Does society determine it in an arbitrary way or is society guided by some objective facts? Are positive laws of society mere expressions of the arbitrary will of authority or are positive laws the expression of intrinsic and objective morality?

If morality is not made by an outside factor, but is discovered in the very nature of an act, how do we discover it? What is the criterion or norm that will indicate for us whether an act is good or bad?

All these questions constitute the problem of the *criterion or norm of morality.* As we have seen in the analysis of the term *good,* the reaching of the fullness of a being is generally considered good. Thus, reaching the totality of one's humanity would be the true human good, and an action which helps us toward the completion of our humanity would be the truly good action. The truly human good, perfecting us in our humanity, and not just in some particular skill or aspect of our humanity, is called the moral good. We are not complete and perfect in our humanity when we are born, but we try to achieve the perfection of our nature throughout our life by performing acts which contribute to this perfection.

But what is the perfection of man? Almost all ethicians, from ancient times to the present, declare either implicitly or explicitly that all men strive to achieve happiness. Happiness, then, would be the perfection of man. Happiness, however, admits of different, even contradictory, interpretations. It is a subjective state produced by the possession of some particular thing. The question, then, has to move to the consideration of those objects or actions which produce happiness. We cannot aim directly at happiness, but rather we have to seek objects the possession of which results in the fulfillment of man and produces happiness.

Ethicians, then, have to concentrate their investigation on the nature of the acts which improve man in his humanity and thus bring about some form of happiness.

All ethical systems propose some criterion or norm that makes the act conducive to improvement in the humanity of a person. Ethical systems differ from one another by the norms they profess and the arguments they use to prove the validity of their norms of morality.

The Method of Our Search for a Valid Criterion of Morality

We will examine the different criteria or norms applied to this question by the major ethical systems developed in history and still held today by various groups, either philosophically expressed or implicitly proclaimed by their conduct. Every student of ethics has the personal task to examine which one of the criteria can be proved valid. In other words, it is our personal duty to search rationally for that factor in an action that makes it good or bad, and to establish our own well reasoned norm of morality. We can be helped in this task, but ultimately it is a personal rational judgment for which we bear the responsibility as we have to be intellectually honest in this search.

VII
Criteria of Morality

In a brief systematic presentation of the main principles of ethics, we cannot review all the ethical theories which have been developed throughout history. We shall only consider four major types of ethics as relevant to our search for a valid criterion of morality.

Ethical systems can be classified in different ways and it is only for the sake of clarity, as a help for our investigation, that we divide them into four major groups, without insisting that this is the only possible classification. Some ethical systems could even be placed in two different groups, depending on what aspect of the system is emphasized and given greater importance.

The *first* group questions our ability to prove in a rational way whether an act is good or bad. It does not produce any rational criterion of morality but holds that moral statements have their origin in emotions.

The *second* group affirms that we can recognize the moral good but cannot give any reason of why an act is held good or bad because good and bad are ultimate, irreducible qualities or categories. We know good and bad intuitively.

The *third* group places the criterion of morality in elements which are outside an act. Thus it proposes an extrinsic morality, which may become subjective if the extrinsic forces that determine morality can change in an arbitrary way.

The *fourth* group claims to find the criterion of morality in the nature of an act, that is, in the ability of an act to promote a certain goal which, in most cases, is the fulfillment of man in his humanity. According to this theory, morality is intrinsic and objective because it depends on the objective characteristics of the human act.

I. The Emotive Theory

The followers of the Emotive Theory hold that ethical statements or moral-value statements are meaningless. There can be no way of knowing whether they are true or false. Value judgments are expressions of emotions.

The main representative of this theory is *Alfred Jules Ayer* (b. 1910). He based his doctrine on the epistemological principles of the so-called Vienna Circle. The members of this group, mostly scientists interested in philosophy, developed the school of logical positivism in the early 1920's. Ayer, after graduating from Oxford University, studied logical positivism in Vienna and, returning to England, constructed his emotive theory of ethics, based on the principles of logical positivism.

According to Ayer, there are only two kinds of meaningful statements: analytic statements and empirical statements. In an analytical statement the predicate is contained in the subject and consequently we do not gain any new knowledge from it. These are statements, for instance, of logic and mathematics which do not describe the world. They are verified by an appeal to other meanings and by deductive reasoning. Examples are: "the whole is larger than its parts"; "three times four is equal to twelve." Empirical statements add something new to our knowledge because the predicate affirms something which cannot be deduced from the meaning of the subject. Empirical statements are verified by sense experience and the refined modern methods of the sciences, which are ultimately based on experience.

In the opinion of Ayer, moral statements are meaningless because they cannot be verified by either method. They are neither false nor true, but simply meaningless, because they do not describe any state of affairs.[1] There is no difference in meaning between "You have stolen this money" and "You have done wrong in stealing this money." "You have done wrong" adds nothing to the meaning of the simple factual statement.

What, then, are ethical statements? They simply show my feeling, my emotions of liking or disliking. These expressions are not cognitive but emotive. They may also express wishes and exhortations. When I say that something is morally good, I equivalently express my liking for it. When I affirm that something is evil, I simply express my dislike. Moral value is not a part of the real world and consequently no ethical system can be proved to be true or false. Ethics catalogue our likes and dislikes, but cannot give reasons for this listing. Hence the followers of this theory are also called noncognitivists.

Charles L. Stevenson (b. 1908), holds that the emotional meaning of moral statements is not entirely irrational.[2] We can give reasons for our approvals and disapprovals because our likes and dislikes hang together in a logical way. Ethics analyzes this logical coherence of approvals and disapprovals and thus can find some reason for our ethical judgment.

Evaluation. The followers of the emotive school were a relatively small group of mostly Anglo-Saxon philosophers. The theory provoked much criticism and recently has lost its influence in philosophical circles.

The critics of emotivism admit the necessity of careful analysis of all our concepts and acknowledge the contribution of the analytical school of philosophy in its insistence on the distinction between scientific and value judgments.

On the other hand, the critics point out that emotions and attitudes in themselves do not make an act good or bad. Philosophy has to explain the firm belief of a large number of people that some acts are objectively right and others are objectively wrong independent of our emotions. The search for goodness in the realm of moral values is similar to the search for truth in science and a rational investigation is not only justified but imperative for decent human living. As one cannot apply empirical and scientific methods in the field of mathematics, so it would be wrong to apply either mathematical or scientific methods in the realm of morality. Morality is a special part of reality which has to develop its own method of verifying right and wrong.

Further, the emotive theory is refuted by its own criterion. This theory is not an analytical statement, since its predicate is not contained in the subject, nor is it a theory verifiable by experience. Consequently it does not have any legitimate claim to be true according to its own criterion.

II. Intuitionism

The second group we examine deals principally with the way we recognize good or evil in our actions. Good and evil can be known with certitude; most people have an awareness of the morally good or bad in human life. The intuitionists, however, do not offer any objective criterion of morality but affirm that we apprehend the rightness or wrongness of an act by some kind of intuition.

1. Naturalistic Fallacy

George Edward Moore (1873–1958)[3] criticized the traditional ethical systems for their attempt to define the moral good and stated that the concept of good is indefinable. His reason is that all definition is analysis of the concept into its components. The good is, however, a simple concept and cannot be broken down into component parts. Most ethical systems, according to Moore, are trying to define the "good" in terms of something else. The hedonists define good or rather identify it with pleasure, the utilitarians with the useful, other systems with self-realization, self-fulfillment or with the will of God.

Moore argues that all these theories confuse "ethical" facts with "natural" facts and commit the Naturalistic Fallacy. We can define good objects, the natural facts which we hold good, e.g. self-fulfillment, but we cannot define the predicate "good"; we cannot analyze what makes them good.

Moore, however, is not an ethical skeptic, because he holds that we can know the good, since not all knowledge is knowledge through definition. For instance we cannot define the color yellow and yet we know what yellow is. A totally blind or a color-blind person cannot know yellow by definition or description. A person with normal eyesight, however, knows what yellow is without any definition. Similarly we know what the good is without any definition. Goodness is a fact; it is an indefinable quality which is known simply and directly in the way a simple natural quality like yellow is known.

It follows from this that the moral good is known by some kind of intuition. Moore does not hold, however, that we cannot rationally discuss ethics. Just as the physicist can validly state many things about the color yellow, so the ethicist can have a rational discourse about the many aspects and consequences of the moral good. Moore actually developed a certain variety of utilitarianism based on his intuitive theory. He affirmed in his *Ethics*[4] that our duty is to perform actions which produce good.

Evaluation. Many critics of Moore deny his assumption that a thing can only be defined by analysis and that the nature of a thing is determined in no way by the nature of other things. Many things, especially universals, like justice, beauty, faithfulness, goodness, are determined by their relations to other things and universals. Many theories of ethics explain the nature of good by showing the relation of human acts to the totality or fullness of a being and reject the static view of reality that would break it up into small unanalyzable components. The parts of reality are interconnected in a dynamic scheme and their relation to one another is a reality which adds something to the nature of the parts. For instance, society is a reality and it cannot be defined by describing the individuals who make up society because society is more than a mere sum-total of individuals. The dynamic interrelationship of the members produces a special being which differs from a rush hour crowd in the street where people have no particular permanent interrelationship. The dynamic intentional union of the individuals for a common goal is the essential element that transforms a group of individuals into a society. Similarly, justice is understood as the dynamic relationship of two or more persons who are obliged to give one another their respective rights.

2. The Moral Sense Theory

a. Anthony Ashley Cooper, third earl of *Shaftesbury* (1671–1713), a British "gentleman philosopher," was probably the first to express clearly the principles of the moral sense school. In his books[5] he proposes virtue or moral goodness as the result of a proper balance between the "natural kindly or generous affections" and the "unnatural affections" of hatred and hostility. In order to achieve the proper balance we must recognize the positive or negative values of these affections. He states that we easily distinguish between hostile and kindly treatment from early childhood and are attracted by the latter and repelled by the former. He calls the faculty by which we make the distinction the "moral sense." It seems that this moral sense is a feeling of attraction or repulsion, similar to our attraction and repulsion by beauty or ugliness in the realm of aesthetics. The moral sense is a reflex moral sensibility, which is the reason for our deliberate choice of the right or wrong course of action.

b. *Joseph Butler* (1692–1752), Anglican bishop of Bristol, argued[6] that there are three principles which motivate men in their moral life: the principle of benevolence, the principle of self-love and the principle of reflection. Reflection is exercised by a "moral approval and disapproval faculty" which may be called "conscience, moral sense or Divine Reason." It could also be considered as "a sentiment of understanding."

c. *Francis Hutcheson* (1694–1747),[7] affirms that we have an immediate intuition of beauty, without any rational calculation. He states that we similarly perceive moral beauty intuitively. The moral sense is an "internal sense," and it regulates and controls our actions.

d. *Adam Smith* (1723–1790), is better known for his famous *Wealth of Nations* (1776), than for his earlier work *Theory of Moral Sentiments* (1759).[8] He was professor of philosophy at Glasgow and belonged to the school that postulated some special sense to apprehend the moral good. He spoke of the sense of propriety by which we know the moral good. This sense of propriety is a kind of "impartial spectator" in us. Impartiality can be achieved if we examine our conduct as if it were someone else's. We will approve or disapprove of our own conduct according to our sympathy or antipathy with the sentiments which are prompted by our actions. This sense of propriety can be called conscience and it is an instinctive sentiment of sympathy.

Evaluation. Reflecting on our reactions to cases of injustice, cruelty, deception or kindness, helping others, etc., it is easy to come to the conclusion, as the moral sense school does, that we have an instinctive sympathy for the good and antipathy for the evil. The followers of this school are engaged in a detailed analysis of these emotions and affections, and conclude that there must be a moral sense or some faculty that prompts these reactions.

The critics point out that the origin of these affections can be explained without presupposing the existence of a moral sense. We are taught by our parents, the school and society to avoid certain actions as evil and perform others as good. All our judgments and actions are accompanied in some way by feelings but we should note that the judgment is the product of reasoning and not of feeling. These two operations, reasoning and feeling, should not be confused. As we grow up and repeat the judgments we learned in our childhood, it will be natural that we will be repelled by cruelty and injustice, especially if it happens to us, and attracted by kindness and good will.

The judgment on the morality of an act is, however, ultimately the product of reasoning and not the result of feeling. Psychology has been unable to find any so-called moral sense or special faculty, the function of which would be to provide us with the knowledge of good and evil. Rather, it is our intellect that pronounces on the rightness or wrongness of an action as it quickly applies certain principles to concrete cases. Conscience is not an instinctive sentiment of sympathy, but the practical reasoning of our intellect.

Furthermore, basing the knowledge of good and evil on sentiments could not give a solid basis to moral life because sentiments change and emotional mood would be a relativistic basis for morality.

III. Theories Proposing Extrinsic Criteria

1. Moral Positivism

The third group finds the origin and explanation of morality in some factors which are extrinsic to the act. These external forces can be the power of a central authority or government, the influence or will of strong men, the opinion of the majority or social pressure, the interests of the ruling class, or the arbitrarily free will of God as he imposes his laws on mankind.

This theory has found many followers throughout history, and there are many persons today who consciously, or by force of habit, accept the "way of life" of a given society or social class as the norm of their moral conduct. As social customs change, so does morality in their opinion, because good and evil are determined by shifting public opinion or varying circumstances.

2. Social Contract Theories

Thomas Hobbes (1588–1679), was a systematic philosopher and emphasized the practical purpose of philosophy. We can find three systems of ethics in his writings, and the one that expresses the moral positivist view most clearly is explained in his *Leviathan, or the Matter, Form, and Power of a Commonwealth, Ecclesiastical and Civil* (1651).

Hobbes describes the origin of society and asserts that before the formation of civil society men were in a constant state of war with one another. Man is an aggressive and antisocial being and in his original state there was a war of all against all. Men fear death above everything, however, and realizing that they cannot achieve safety alone, form a civil society and unconditionally consent to the rule of government. The central authority imposes rules and laws, and the concepts of good and evil are introduced for the first time by these laws prohibiting or prescribing certain actions. The source of good and evil in this theory is the will of the government, which is extrinsic to an act, and thus the norm of morality becomes a positive factor determining rightness and wrongness from without. It follows directly from this theory that might is right.

According to Hobbes, the original social contract had to be an unconditional consent to the rule of authority because otherwise the subjects could reserve the right to disobey the laws of society and eventually they would return to the previous state of war. The guarantee of political authority against violence and a chaotic existence is the reason why governments have power to issue orders and determine the rightness and wrongness of actions. Consequently morality is conventional and is not determined by the nature of an act.

Jean Jacques Rousseau (1712–1778), explains, in his *Social Contract* (1762), how human society and the laws regulating our conduct came into being. Unlike Hobbes, he thinks that men in the "state of nature" did what was naturally good and were not in a state of war against one another.

Nevertheless, he accepted the basic premise that men are selfish by nature and affirmed that self-interest was transformed into moral obligation by the social contract. The basis of the social contract is the General Will, i.e., the collective will of the members of society to obey the laws imposed upon them by political authority for the sake of peace, orderly life and the common good. This transition from the state of nature to the civil state is the origin of morality.

Rousseau tries to avoid the extreme position of moral positivism when he insists that, obeying the general will, we actually obey ourselves and thus remain free. Nevertheless, he admits that authority has to coerce the selfish man to comply with his "real" will, "forcing him to become free." This is obviously a rather peculiar interpretation of human freedom. It would be more logical to say that political authority imposes the law of conduct upon the members of society.

3. The Will of the Strong Man

Friedrich Nietzsche (1844–1900), in his *"Genealogy of Morals: An Attack"* (1887), attributes the origin of the concept of good and evil to the domination of the strong men over the weak. The masters were beyond good and evil but, imposing their will on the slaves, they became the object of the criticism of the oppressed, who called the actions of the masters evil. This fact was the origin of master-morality and slave-morality. Judaism and Christianity took the side of the slaves, the weak, the humble and the poor and propagated the slave-morality under which we now live. The duty of humanity is to restore master-morality, the dominant morality once again and develop the "Übermensch," the "Superman," the aristocracy of the human race who, rising above the common herd, will assure a better future for mankind. The superman is beyond good and evil and his will is the law.

4. Public Opinion, Social Pressure

Public opinion polls have become part of our life. They are gaining more and more importance in political campaigns and many other aspects of modern life. Opinion polls are only one method of studying society and the way men live. *Auguste Comte* (1798–1857), a French positivist philosopher, is considered to have originated the science of sociology which is a positive science that studies the structure, the organization and the development of people living together in social groups.

Some sociologists, transgressing from their positive science to philosophy, identify morality with the ways of life and the customs of the majority. Ethics, in this sense, would become a positive science measuring and registering public opinion and the consensus of the majority. Consequently, morality would become relative and would depend on the shifting opinion of social groups. Changes of moral conduct could be the result of social pressures, the manipulation of society by shrewd men, by the media, and could also be caused by economic development or dislocations, or any other factor that shapes public opinion.

5. *The Will of God*

Samuel von Pufendorf (1632–1694), a Protestant philosopher, is one of the most explicit representatives of this school. According to him, an act is good because God willed it to be so and bad because God condemned it. This theory is called Divine Moral Positivism, because it holds that it is the will of God that determines the rightness or wrongness of an action and not the nature of the act; that is, the determining factor is an extrinsic and positive element.

Von Pufendorf held that God's will is made known to us by revelation. His ethics, however, is not simply a theology of revelation, for he gives it a philosophical interpretation in his great work, *The Law of Nature and of Nations* (1672).

Evaluation. The doctrines listed above are usually called moral positivist theories because they derive morality from the positive laws or customs of society. The moral positivist attitude, both in individual, national and international morality, was well entrenched until World War II. During the last century, natural law ethics, an ethics that bases morality on human nature, came into disrepute for various reasons. Some defenders of natural law morality were partly to blame for this because they interpreted human nature in a static and almost mechanistic way. To a greater degree, however, absolutist and totalitarian tendencies were responsible for creating an atmosphere for the easy acceptance of positivist theories both in jurisprudence and private life.

The great changes caused by the war, however, set in motion all kinds of movements which question the authority of governments to legislate in an arbitrary way. These movements appeal to a fundamental concept of justice and a deeper understanding of right and wrong. The restlessness of the 1960's in the U.S. and many European countries revealed that, in the opinion of many persons, the government is not the source of morality but rather civil authority must respect a fundamental justice which is not based on the will of human authority. Civil disobedience is grounded on the opinion that right and wrong are not an arbitrary creation of a government or even of the majority of the people, but are based on the nature and inherent dignity of man, a dignity that may not be violated by civil authority.

It would be a mistake, however, to consider moral positivism as a theory and practice of the past. A great number of people today follow the majority opinion or the prevailing social customs in their morality. As mores and fads change, so will the moral attitude of these persons. The mass media of communication will have a great influence on a segment of the population which cannot form a well reasoned moral judgment and is easily moved to follow the crowd or the shrewd political campaigner.

Theories proposing extrinsic criteria implicitly state that morality is made by factors which are outside an act. The elements determining morality can be the following: the authority of the government gained by a social contract, the general will of the people, the opinion of the majority or public opinion, the military or police power of the government to enact and execute laws, social pressure, the will of the rich and powerful, the will of God.

The analysis of these theories uncovers several shortcomings and contradictions. Man is not an antisocial being but is, by his very nature, social. Our natural individual needs are greater than our individual power to satisfy them. Only social cooperation can fulfill man's basic needs. We have to be born into a family, and educated by our parents and teachers. Man's constant drive to know more, learn more and develop a civilization can be achieved only by social cooperation. Man is basically social by the indication of his very nature, notwithstanding the fact that some persons sometimes may behave in an antisocial way.

Considering the procedure of making laws, we find that legislators, even in an authoritarian state, must examine the quality of acts or rules to be prescribed from the viewpoint of whether they can achieve the goal of the well-being of society, at least as the legislators understand that well-being. In other words, the rightness or wrongness of an act is determined by some quality within the act. Hearings are conducted and experts are consulted to ascertain that the acts to be prescribed by the law have the quality by which a certain goal can be reached. Murder is judged to be wrong, not because society forbids it, but it is held wrong by its very nature. Society forbids it because it is wrong before any legislation. No society could survive that would arbitrarily decide the rightness or wrongness of actions.

Similarly the opinion of the majority is based on some correct or false understanding of the ability of an act or a type of behavior to achieve some goals. Public opinion is formed slowly by the accumulation of individual convictions that certain actions are good or bad because they lead to some desired goal or prevent us from reaching it.

Some God-fearing persons are of the mistaken opinion that because God is perfectly free, he freely and arbitrarily determines the rightness or wrongness of actions. Sound natural theology holds that God is not free in this sense but is bound by metaphysical laws and the laws of contradiction, of truth and falsehood. We understand these laws because the world is, in a certain sense, a participation in the perfections of God. Through creation it imitates the nature of God. God, as the source of truth, cannot become involved in contradiction. He forbids certain acts because they are bad in themselves, and they do not become evil by God's prohibition.

IV. Theories Proposing Intrinsic Criteria

From the many theories in this group, we will mention only those which were significant in history and are still influential in shaping the moral judgment of many persons.

1. The Principle of Universality

This principle assumes that what is right or wrong for one person would be right or wrong for any person under similar circumstances. It is expressed in the early moral education of children, for instance, when their parents tell them not to hurt their brothers or sisters because they certainly don't want to be hurt by them. "Don't hurt him; he is not hurting you."

It is also expressed in the *Golden Rule:* "Treat others as you would like to be treated by them."

It has to be noted that the principle of universality does not really consider the content of the moral law but only the form into which an act has to fit in order to be held good. In one sense, then, we could say that it does not give an intrinsic criterion of morality. In another sense, however, the characteristic or intrinsic quality of the act has to be taken into consideration when one tries to fit it into the universal form. The difficulty is that there is no clear guiding principle given about how one can make this fitting, about what kind of concrete qualities the act must have for this.

The moral philosophy of *Immanual Kant* (1724–1804), although quite sophisticated in its justification and presentation, can ultimately be reduced to the principle of universality. Kant's epistemological theory holds that our "pure reason" cannot know the "thing in itself," that is, the essence or noumenon of beings, but only the appearance or phenomenon of things. Our "practical reason," however, accepts a number of postulates because we simply cannot lead a moral life without accepting certain truths.

One of the truths our practical reason recognizes is the existence and the universal character of moral obligation. Different societies or different persons throughout history may have lived according to different moral laws, but they all agreed on the main characteristic of those laws, namely, that they should be universally obeyed. The "form" of the moral law is that it imposes an obligation without any condition; it is a *categorical imperative*. The matter or the content of the law varies, but the important aspect of the moral law is that it has a universal claim, and this does not vary. The universality or the form of the law should give stability and permanence also to the content of the law if the form is applied critically to the content. Hence Kant concludes that the criterion of morality is the principle: "Act only on the maxim whereby you can at the same time will that it should become a universal law." Since, according to the epistemological theory of Kant, the pure reason cannot perceive the ontological order of nature, the practical formula of the universality of the law should guide us in our moral deliberations. Thus, the categorical imperative is an empty shell or form without real content. This is the reason why Kant's moral theory is called *ethical formalism*. In forming a moral judgment, we should always apply this form to our actions, "What would happen if everybody did that?" or "Could I wish that everybody in the same situation should act as I plan to act?"

Evaluation. Almost all religions propose the Golden Rule in some form as the practical guide to morality. One should not deny that it is a convenient rule of thumb which in many situations is helpful. But the principle of universality in itself does not give an answer to the question why certain acts are good and others are bad because it does not analyze the content of the act, at least not explicitly. It considers only the formula of universalism. A philosophical theory, however, should go beyond the form and should be able to analyze the content of an obligation and offer a reason why a certain type of action is good or bad and why, consequently, such acts should be universally commanded or forbidden.

It seems that it is impossible to arrive at a consideration of universal obligation without trying to give at least some reason why the action should be universally commanded. We cannot declare for universality without first examining the content of the law, that is, the nature of the act which is commanded or forbidden. This investigation will somehow indicate that an act is good or bad because it leads to or prevents the reaching of a necessary goal of human existence, e.g., the development of man as a rational and social being. Thus truthfulness should be a universal law because it is necessary for human cooperation, without which we could not satisfy even our basic physical and intellectual needs.

The principle of universality considers some characteristics of an act, namely, the quality enabling it to become a universal law. Hence the theory offers a criterion of morality which is intrinsic to the act in some way. But this quality of universality is not explained further. No clear objective reason is given to prove why the act should be universally commanded or forbidden. The lack of some objective justification could lead to opening the door for subjective interpretations of morality. What usually happens, however, in the application of this principle of universality, is the abandonment of the theory itself, because most people try to prove by objective reasons why the act should be universally prescribed or forbidden. In other words, they go beyond the empty form of the categorical imperative and undertake an analysis of the nature of the act.

2. Hedonism

The Greek word, "hédoné," means pleasure. Hedonism is an ethical system that holds pleasure to be the norm of morality. The Greek philosopher, *Aristippus of Cyrene* (ca. 435–ca. 356 B.C.), maintained that pleasure is the only good and identified happiness with pleasure. The good act is that which brings sense pleasure, either directly or indirectly, i.e., as a means to pleasure, and the bad act is that which results in pain or unpleasant feelings. The goal of man is happiness and happiness consists of pleasure. Hence, the moral goodness of an act is determined by the property of its ability to produce pleasure; i.e., morality consists in some intrinsic quality of an act insofar as it is a means to the goal of human life.

Aristippus and the Cyrenaics emphasized sense pleasure over intellectual pleasure because it is more intense and more gratifying, hence more conducive to happiness. The wise man, however, that is, the philosopher, will not pursue pleasure indiscriminately and to excess, because that would lead to pain and not to enjoyment. Man has to exercise some self-control lest he become a slave of pleasure which would be a painful experience. It follows from this that the wise man must limit his desires and keep a proper balance in his life in order to achieve the highest enjoyment and the greatest happiness in life.

Epicurus (341–270 B.C.), like the Cyrenaics, identified the goal of life with pleasure. Whereas the Cyrenaics emphasized the pleasure of the present,

Epicurus preferred pleasures that endure. Since sense pleasure is not enduring, he taught that the goal of man is rational pleasure, which consists mainly in tranquillity of soul, peace of mind and harmonious living in society. Virtue is valued as a means to produce intellectual pleasure. Self-control is an apt means to produce enduring pleasures, and so is friendship and wisdom. Acts which are capable of increasing our peace of mind, or intellectual pleasure, are the morally good acts, and anything that causes pain or anxiety is a morally bad act and should be avoided.

Evaluation. A person's acceptance or rejection of these theories will evidently depend on his understanding of the goal of man. Is the purpose of human life sense or intellectual pleasure, or is there something more that gives meaning to human existence?

In addition to the question of the basic orientation of man, critics point out that hedonists equate pleasure with the good without offering convincing reasons; the equation is assumed as self-evident. It is true that pleasure is desired in some way, but it is not evident that every object of our desire is good. Many actions are universally held good, and yet they do not produce pleasure, or at least not sense pleasure. Honesty and truthfulness are good even if they can be achieved only through sacrifices and hard work. The constant pursuit of sense pleasure is unworthy of a rational being, and it is a well-known psychological fact that such a pursuit does not bring happiness but rather, boredom and dissatisfaction. Pleasure often means a short time of pleasant feeling without long-lasting satisfaction.

The philosophy of Epicurus is more refined than the doctrine of the Cyrenaics because it takes into consideration the spiritual and rational characteristics of man. Nevertheless, it does not prove its basic tenet that intellectual pleasure and good are interchangeable terms and mean the same thing.

3. *Utilitarianism*

The philosophy of utilitarianism is based upon the doctrine that the only motives of human actions are pleasure and pain, the former prompting us to perform an act, the other compelling man to avoid an action. According to this theory, a psychological analysis of our actions reveals the fact that we necessarily seek pleasure and try to avoid pain. This theory is called psychological hedonism, i.e., it explains the *reality* of man, as distinguished from moral or ethical hedonism, which teaches that man *ought* to seek pleasure.

The philosophy of utilitarianism developed in England in the 18th and 19th centuries. Its main exponents were the British philosophers, Jeremy Bentham and John Stuart Mill.

Jeremy Bentham (1748–1832) lived in a turbulent era of political revolutions, wars and the beginning of the industrial revolution. Early in his life, he became interested in honest government and the general reform of society. His philosophy of utilitarianism is best explained in his *Introduction to the Principles of Morals and Legislation* (1789). Being a prolific writer, references to his utilitarian theories are found also in his legal and political writings.

Bentham's starting point is the description of psychological hedonism. All men act to gain pleasure or to avoid pain. Man is selfish and will not act unless to procure his own pleasure. Sometimes he may promote his own advantage by serving others, but even in this case the motive is a selfish interest and not the good of others. In his description of the psychology of man, he identifies pleasure with happiness and concludes that the first principle of ethics is that the right and desirable goal of human action is happiness, that is, pleasure and the avoidance of pain.

He holds that this first principle is self-evident and needs no proof. It follows from this that the rightness or wrongness of an act has to be judged by its consequences and by the ability of the act to produce pleasure or remove pain. An action that produces a mixture of pleasure and pain has to be judged according to the quantity of pleasure or pain. Whichever is greater will give the action its moral character. When one has a choice among various actions producing pleasure, the wise decision is the one that selects the act resulting in the greatest pleasure or greatest happiness. Pleasure and happiness are taken as synonyms.

He calls the property of any act or object that produces pleasure or happiness "utility." Hence the theory is commonly called utilitarianism.

There are different kinds of pleasure, like eating and drinking, listening to music or looking at beautiful paintings; but according to Bentham, pleasures can be measured quantitatively; they can be reduced to units of pleasure, and so it becomes possible to calculate the magnitude of happiness. Since man seeks pleasure and tries to avoid pain by psychological necessity, the proper goal of conscious human actions is to act in such a way that the greatest happiness is achieved. It seems implied in the theory of Bentham that we are free in choosing among different quantities of pleasure or happiness, and thus the moral law would mean the obligation to seek the greatest happiness. Consequently, ethical hedonism is derived from psychological hedonism.

The *greatest happiness* principle may refer to individuals or to the community. If we think of the community, we have to strive with our actions for the greatest happiness of the greatest number of people. The greatest happiness of the greatest number of people is the goal of the community, and a good government should promote this common good.

A contradiction seems to be present here between the egoistic utilitarianism of Bentham and his principle of the greatest happiness of the greatest number of people. A solution is given in his suggestion that if an individual acts without concern for the common good, he will suffer painful consequences, and thus he will act against the principle of his own greatest happiness. Consequently, one promotes the common good only out of enlightened self-interest.

If we can gauge pleasure accurately, ethics, in the opinion of Bentham, becomes an exact science. To achieve this goal, he proposed the *felicific or hedonistic* calculus. The application of this calculus gives us the precise degree of the magnitude of pleasure. There are seven factors to be measured in any act: intensity, duration, certainty, propinquity, fecundity, purity and extent. Some of these factors need a brief explanation. Fecundity means the ability of an act to generate more pleasure. Purity indicates that the pleasure is not mixed with pain. Extent signifies here the number of persons who are affected by the pleasure or pain when we consider the common good.

Although Bentham did not use the terms of Act-Utilitarianisms and Rule-Utilitarianism, these more recent concepts can be basically deduced from his theory.

Act-Utilitarianism examines the utility of individual acts in terms of whether they promote the greatest happiness of the individual or the greatest happiness of the greatest number of people.

Rule-Utilitarianism, on the other hand, considers universal laws and examines the utility of these laws or rules in terms of whether they promote the greatest happiness of the greatest number of people.

Act-Utilitarianism, in a certain sense, resembles modern situation ethics. It is the individual act in its particular and concrete situation that is considered and examined to see whether it produces the greatest balance of good over evil in the world. The morality of the act is determined by its unique relationship to the consequences of the act and not by its relationship to a general rule. For instance, the question may be asked whether telling a falsehood in a particular case will produce a greater amount of happiness than telling the truth. If it does produce a greater amount of happiness all around, then telling a falsehood in this particular situation is the right way of acting according to Act-Utilitarianism.

Rule-Utilitarianism, on the other hand, resembles the ethical theory of universality. Here the emphasis is on general rules of morality and not on particular situations. In determining the rules of morality the guiding principle is that the rule which produces the greatest general good for all is the rule of morality obliging everybody in all circumstances of life. Exceptions in individual cases are not allowed because the permission to make exceptions ultimately would disturb the social order and so even the person using the exception for his own benefit would be hurt more than helped by this exception. The rule-utilitarian, just as the universalist, has to ask the question: What would happen if everybody acted as I do? Would the act produce a balance of good over evil in the world?

Both forms of utilitarianism insist that the utility of the act to promote the greatest happiness of the greatest number of people determines the morality of the act. One has to note, however, that rule-utilitarianism resorts also to the principle of universality. Furthermore, it has to apply also the principle of justice in determining the morality of a rule. The reason is that a certain rule can produce the greatest amount of good in a society but, at the same time, it can violate the equitable and just distribution of this good, and it can suppress or exploit the minority in favor of the majority. It is evident that a rule is not morally right if it only intends to maximize the amount of good and does not provide for the equitable and just distribution of this amount of good. But the consideration of justice in formulating rules means the abandonment of the principles of utilitarianism.[8a]

Since both forms of utilitarianism are built upon the principle of utility, the following evaluation applies to both.

Evaluation. The following are some of the remarks offered by critics of utilitarianism.

According to Bentham, it is a psychological fact that we necessarily seek pleasure and avoid pain. It does not make much sense, however, to state that we ought to seek pleasure and ought to avoid pain when we necessarily do so. He describes the fact of man's tendency but does not explain the oughtness of moral obligation.

The first principle of utilitarianism, that we always seek pleasure and try to avoid pain, was proposed as self-evident, but it does not seem to be true that all our conscious and deliberate acts always seek pleasure.

Pleasure is identified with happiness without sufficient proof, as was pointed out above in connection with hedonism.

If it is proposed that the criterion of morality is that property of an act which produces happiness, the goal of the action becomes even more vague and undetermined than is the case with pleasure. The nature of happiness is not explained adequately. It is simply supposed that everybody seeks happiness and understands what it is. But it is difficult, if not entirely impossible, to arrive at a commonly accepted understanding of happiness. Who is going to determine, for instance, what the happiness of the community should be? Will it be the government, the head of the state, the majority of the people? All answers would create great problems. Furthermore, happiness cannot be aimed at directly, because it is the by-product of the conscious possession of some object of our desire or of the performance of some acts.

Utility is a term used by Bentham in a sense different from ordinary usage. Generally it means usefulness or refers to a means to achieve some end. Bentham uses it exclusively for that quality of an act that produces happiness.

The hedonistic calculus does not work in practice. It is impossible to calculate the quantity of happiness that should be the result of an action in the case of an individual. When the question concerns the greatest happiness of the greatest number of people, the calculation of the sum total of happiness becomes even more difficult since many members of a community will not agree as to what happiness means for them. If Bentham meant only to give us a rough guideline in his hedonistic calculus, one could agree that such a rough appraisal is possible in individual cases. Some people evidently make such estimates. But if this was the intention of Bentham, he abandoned his goal of making ethics into an exact science.

John Stuart Mill (1806–1873), came under the influence of Bentham to such a degree that utilitarianism became his religion. Later, in his *Utilitarianism* he defended the basic ideas of Bentham but also improved upon the doctrine.

Mill accepted the greatest happiness principle of Bentham and agreed with him that man seeks pleasure and tries to avoid pain in all his actions. Happiness is the goal of human life and happiness is identified with pleasure.

While approving the basic tenets of Bentham's utilitarianism, Mill rejects his opinion that pleasures differ from one another only in quantity. Mill maintains that pleasures differ also qualitatively, that there **are** lower and higher types of pleasure. A good man "would rather be a human being dissatisfied than a pig satisfied; rather be Socrates dissatisfied than a fool satisfied."[9]

In addition to the qualitative classification of pleasures, Mill emphasized the social character of happiness. One has to seek the greatest happiness of the greatest number of people. The end of moral action is not merely one's own happiness but the greatest amount of happiness of all.

Evaluation. Mill has greatly improved upon the utilitarianism of Bentham and by the introduction of qualitative differences in pleasures and the emphasis on social concern, made it more respectable.

Nevertheless, his identification of pleasure with the moral good remained unproved, just as in the theory of Bentham. Neither is the transition from psychological hedonism to ethical hedonism proved. The fact that men do seek pleasure is a factual statement. It does not follow from it that men *should* seek pleasure in all their actions. Furthermore, if psychological hedonism is true, namely, that we seek pleasure in all our actions, the obligation that we should do so does not make much sense. There are good reasons, however, to doubt the universal validity of psychological hedonism.

In addition, there is some inconsistency in the utilitarianism of Mill. While he affirms that happiness or pleasure is the highest good and the criterion of morality, he admits that it is better to be a human being dissatisfied than a pig satisfied. It seems that Mill here implicitly considers human nature as the criterion of morality. Unfortunately, he did not elaborate his understanding of human nature clearly, but he suggests that "true" human nature is the criterion of morality for him when he states that it is better to be Socrates dissatisfied than a fool satisfied. This is even better expressed when he discusses the principle of the greatest happiness of the greatest number of people. He derives this principle from the social nature of man as he concludes that man is obliged by his very nature to promote the common good.

Utilitarians who aim at the greatest happiness of all people must assume, at least implicitly, some idea of the universal character of human nature and of the ways in which this nature is fulfilled. Without presupposing what man really is by his nature, one cannot realistically propose any reform to improve the life of man in society. Hence it seems that all utilitarians implicitly go beyond their admitted norm of pleasure and arrive at human nature as the criterion of morality.

4. Theories of Self-Realization — The Fulfillment of Potentialities

Followers of self-realization ethical theories span two and a half millennia, and it is probable that this type of theory has the most adherents among both philosophers and the man in the street. That is, if we take into consideration its various forms and the implicit acceptance of its essential traits by specific theories listed under different names.

The common element in all self-realization theories is the doctrine that moral good for the individual consists in the development of one's potentialities as perfectly as possible, and thus the fulfilling or realizing of one's nature. This fulfillment is achieved by actualizing the potentialities of man in a harmonious way, considering all the important elements of human nature, including the inherent social character of man.

Plato (ca. 429–347 B.C.), based his ethics on his theory of knowledge and his metaphysics. For Plato it is thought, and not sense perception, that really apprehends the essence of objects. An example would be "the understanding of beauty." We call various objects beautiful. Since we discover beauty in various things, the idea of beauty itself must have some reality because otherwise we would not be able to apprehend it. We do not invent the reality of beauty but understand it when it is presented to us. The same analysis is valid for the idea of the good and for other universals. Plato thought it quite logical to hold that there is a reality to absolute goodness and absolute beauty. Goodness and beauty in different objects are the reflection of and participation in the "ideal form" of absolute goodness and absolute beauty. It was only one further step for Plato to expand the theory of ideal forms to all objects and not limit it to moral and aesthetic universals. Thus the world of our sense perception is only the reflection of the true world of ideal forms. The world of ideal forms is inhabited by an eternal and perfect archetype of every species of thing. All beings on this earth participate in an ideal form. So man, too, shares in the ideal form of humanity. Universal ideas, then, have real ontological existence and are not merely abstractions of our mind.

Our intellect connects us to the universal forms, to this real world. Consequently, the mind is the most important aspect of man, representing his true self. Man is really man through his mind.

Plato did not deny the importance of pleasure, because for him man is not exclusively intellectual. The good life for man must consist in developing his true nature, resembling more and more the ideal form of humanity. Since man is not just mind, the good life must consist of harmoniously combined activities of the mind and of the senses. While we live in this mortal life, we must always realize that this is not the true world, but only a copy of the perfect world of ideal forms. Moral goodness consists in trying to resemble the perfect world as much as we can by developing our potentialities, especially by increasing our knowledge. The knowledge of the perfect Good is important for man to be able to fulfill his nature and to achieve happiness, which will be complete only in our return to the realm of the perfect world from which our soul was taken at our birth, becoming imprisoned in our body.

In his *Republic*, Plato describes the ideal state, in which man is capable of developing and living harmoniously, that is, is helped to live a morally good life. He emphasizes the social nature of man and consequently the criterion of morality for him would be the dynamic and social nature of man as it is developing and becoming fulfilled in society and through social cooperation. Harmonious living in society will aid man to approach the perfect Good. The goal of man is to resemble the perfect Good as much as possible. Sharing the perfections of the highest Good will bring happiness to man. The goal of man, therefore, is to achieve happiness by sharing in the being of the Absolute.

Aristotle (384–322 B.C.). The ethics of Aristotle is based on his metaphysics, which rejects Plato's theory of a separate world of ideal forms. Nevertheless, Aristotle agreed with Plato that there must be a reality that corresponds to the universal ideas or essences of beings. There must be something real that makes gold gold, a horse a horse, a man a human being. The universal idea or essence of things, however, cannot exist separately, but must be realized in individual beings. The essence of a being makes it what it is. He called the universal essence as realized in the individual, the *substantial form* of beings. This form could be called nature since it is the source of the specific activities of a being. It determines the way a being exists and operates. We do not see this form or source of operations, but we conclude to its reality from the observation of a being. "As a being is so it acts." An apple tree bears apples and not pears; an eagle flies and does not swim like a fish; gold does not rust like iron, etc. From the effects, that is, from the operations of a being, we conclude to the existence of the cause of operations. This reality, which could be called the nature of a being, determines its activities.

Substantial forms do not exist separately or in themselves, but they are the constitutive factors in each existing individual of the same class of beings. Every person is a human being, has the essence or nature of humanity, but humanity as such does not exist separately. The specific essence of a being is *numerically* different in each individual of the same species, but it is *essentially* the same in all members of the species. Universal ideas only exist in our minds; they are abstractions. But these ideas have an objective foundation in existing individuals as all these individuals are really and objectively either dogs, or horses, or human beings, etc.

Trying to understand the fact of change and growth in living beings, the concept of substantial form became a key element for the philosophy of Aristotle in explaining life. There is an unchangeable, dynamic core in a constantly changing being. The fully developed oak tree is the same thing it basically was in the acorn, and yet it is different from it. Aristotle uses the comparison of a sculptor changing a block of marble into a statue. The sculptor adds the form of the statue to the marble. Here the form is added from without and by an external agent. Form and matter are united and become a specific statue. The substantial form, in natural objects, however, operates within a being. It remains the same form or essence, and it determines a changing and passive element, which Aristotle called *prime matter*. Prime matter, however, cannot exist separately from the form, just as the substantial form cannot exist separately. In any existing being the form is already united with prime matter and gives the being its specific character or nature.

In living beings or in any organic growth, the substantial form organizes the matter. It is the internal principle that causes the growth of a specific being according to the nature or form of that being. Thus an acorn always grows up into an oak tree and not into an apple tree. The form expresses itself in the process of growth and becomes truly what it is by its nature. The oak tree differs from the acorn, and yet the oak tree is virtually in the acorn. In the process of life it becomes fully developed; its potency to become an oak tree is completed, fulfilled. It follows from this that the form is the moving or "formal" cause of life and at the same time it is also the goal, the final cause of a being. A being is truly realized when it reaches the fullness of its nature, the totality of its form. The form in this sense is also the norm according to which a being acts.

All classes of beings, except man, are determined by their form, either physically or psychologically, to act in a specific way. Man alone is free in many of his operations. The full realization of the form or nature, however, remains the goal also for man, the final cause of his life. Aristotle taught that man acts morally when he realizes as fully as possible the potentialities of his substantial form, the ideal of his nature. Since man is a rational animal by nature, he is capable of exploring and understanding his true nature. The good man must seek truth and act according to his true nature. Acts which befit human nature will take man closer to his goal, the achievement of the fullness of his humanity.

Man becomes more fully man and realizes his form, the perfection of his nature, when he acts according to his nature. The proper activity that leads to this realization results in *eudaimonia*, that is, the well-being and happiness of man. The Greek word for goal is *telos* and, since the theory of self-realization means bringing man closer to his goal, this type of ethics is usually called *teleological ethics*.

In a teleological, self-realization theory of ethics, the correct idea of human nature, as the criterion of morality, becomes the basis of the system. Aristotle emphasized the social character of human nature. Man is a social being, and consequently he can achieve the development of his potentialities only through social cooperation in the "polis," in the well organized community. Hence he regarded ethics as part of politics, i.e., the science of organized, harmonious living in society. Human nature for Aristotle is a dynamic source of activities and it cannot be applied to moral problems with a mathematical exactitude. We have to maintain a harmonious balance among our natural drives and tendencies so that human nature is realized in us as fully as possible. Virtues help us to develop our nature and enable us to lead a good and happy life. In his *Nichomachean Ethics*, he presented a highly sensible and practical system of virtues.[10]

St. Thomas Aquinas (ca. 1225–1274), always referred to Aristotle as "The Philosopher" and wrote about him with great respect. He integrated many Aristotelian ideas in his own thoughts and made the philosophy of Aristotle better known in Europe.

St. Thomas was primarily a theologian. Hence he dealt with ethical questions mostly from a theological point of view. His ethical theories, nevertheless, can be easily discerned in his theological writings, especially in the second part of the *Summa Theologica* and in the third book of the *Summa contra Gentiles*. His influence on Christian thinking about morality was considerable not only among his contemporaries but also among succeeding generations.

Aquinas agreed with Aristotle that the morality of a human act is derived from its connection with the final end of man. All beings tend toward the actualization of their potentialities by their very nature and consequently they strive to fulfill their own nature by developing it fully so that they will reach their final end. Man, as a free and intelligent being, strives for his ultimate end, not only by the force of his nature, but also by means of his intellect and will. Rationality and freedom are the foundation upon which the morality of the human act is based. Man can deliberately choose his goal and get closer to it by his actions or can turn against the goal which alone could fulfill him and make him happy. But what is man's ultimate end? Aquinas maintained that no finite object can satisfy man because he reaches beyond finite objects and beyond himself, through his reason and will. St. Thomas, as theologian, asserts that only God can completely satisfy man's desires and the drives of his intellect and will. The supreme good of man is God, but we cannot reach God in this life in a completely satisfying way. Only the *beatific vision* of God in the next life can satisfy us. The beatific vision is an intuitive, intellectual knowledge of God, linking us to the efficient and final cause of our existence. Man, by performing actions that fit his nature, acts morally and thus prepares for his perfect fulfillment of happiness in the next life.

Speaking of the norm of morality, St. Thomas frequently uses the term, "right reason." Since he made intellect the distinguishing characteristic of man, we can understand his emphasis on the activities of the intellect in the matter of morality and happiness. It is through reason that man understands his end and consequently can deliberately and consciously strive for the good. It happens quite frequently, however, that men deliberately choose things which are not objectively good for them and which do not take them closer to their end. "Right reason" grasps the objective good that realizes the potentialities of man and brings him closer to his end. Right reason also considers the particular and concrete circumstances of the agent, his relations to other persons and to society, and chooses what is fitting to man's nature. Reason is right when it judges objectively according to the concrete nature of the agent and chooses actions which objectively fulfill and perfect his nature.

* * * * * *

The three examples of the theories of self-realization we have given here had great influence on ethical thinking through the centuries and gained many adherents. The common element in all self-realization systems is the doctrine that man has a specific nature and that morality consists in performing actions that help man toward the realization of the fullness of his nature. They differ from one another in their metaphysics and philosophy of man, that is, in their understanding of reality in general and the nature of man in particular.

This is the reason why many self-realization

theories place special emphasis on the correct analysis and understanding of human nature. Some especially insist that man should not be taken just as a physical or biological being but should be understood "adequately," as spirit in matter, rational, free and social, who has relations to other human beings and to lesser or greater societies, is marked by interdependence, can influence his own environment, can intervene in his own nature, is "self-manipulating" and self-transcending. He cannot, however, change his own nature completely without ceasing to be a rational and free agent. It is obvious from this consideration that different philosophies of man can result in different criteria of morality within the camp of self-realization theories.

5. *Marxist-Leninist Ethics*

As the term *Christianity* refers to a great variety of Christian doctrines, so does the term *Marxism* cover a fairly large number of different Marxist teachings. Some of these varieties are: Classical Marxism, Neo-Marxism, the New Left, Marxism-Leninism, Marxism-Leninism-Maoism. All forms of Marxism claim to be the legitimate and genuine interpretations or developments of the ideas of Karl Marx. Marx himself left no clearly defined and completed system of thought. Although he strongly condemned the morality of capitalism and the bourgeoisie, his ethics are vague and the problem of morality is not discussed by him explicitly and coherently. The most powerful and influential Marxist theory today is Marxism-Leninism which, in a certain sense, includes also Marxism-Leninism-Maoism. It rules about 40% of the world's population. The great power of this variety of Marxism is the reason why in our brief analysis we will mainly consider Marxism-Leninism.

This doctrine is the official philosophy of Soviet Russia, China and other countries that have installed a communist regime. Most organized communist parties in the West have obediently accepted the Marxist-Leninist doctrine. Recently, however, the Italian and French communist parties proposed some important changes in the doctrine, notably in the theories of the dictatorship of the proletariat and political pluralism. Many observers, however, doubt whether the changes would be introduced into practice if these parties ever came into power.

Lenin was not acquainted with all the writings of Marx and evidently had no access to the writings of the young Marx, which were published at a much later time. Nevertheless, he developed the thoughts of the Marx he knew and made important theoretical and practical contributions to Marxism. Other Soviet leaders and philosophers added their own contributions. The body of Marxist-Leninist philosophy became crystallized around 1950. This philosophy is quite clearly defined in official Soviet publications[11] and is taught as an obligatory and important subject in all schools in communist countries. It claims to be the foundation of the social, political and economic organization of communist countries, as well as the basis of genuine socialist or communist morality. A. F. Shishkin is the author of the official text on Marxist ethics. His book, *Fundamentals of Marxist Ethics*, unfortunately, is not available in English translation.[12]

The ethical theory of Marxism-Leninism is based on its metaphysical doctrine of reality and its philosophy of man. It would go beyond the purpose of this book to explain fully Marxist-Leninist philosophy. Only the outlines of Dialectical and Historical Materialism, the two main parts of Marxist-Leninist philosophy, can be indicated briefly.

Dialectical Materialism, the first part, explains the most basic laws of reality and proposes to prove that everything that exists is either matter or the product of matter. Since matter, according to science, cannot be destroyed, in other words, is indestructible, it is also eternal and uncreatable, which means that there is no Creator. "Nature is its own cause. . . . That materialist formula signifies that nature is in no need of a creator standing above it, that nature itself possesses the attributes of infinity and eternity which the theologians falsely ascribe to God."[13]

The most important and eternal property of matter is motion. Motion, however, must not be taken as only movement in space; it signifies all the various forms of change. Matter is not static but dynamic, and consequently changing. If we can understand the basic laws of material change, we can shed light on the facts of evolution and development in the world. Marxism-Leninism claims that its laws of dialectic, scientifically explain the nature of change. This is the reason why the system is called *Dialectical Materialism*. The three laws of Dialectical Materialism are: 1. The law of transformation of quantitative into qualitative changes and vice versa; 2. The law of unity and struggle of opposites; 3. The law of the negation of negation.[14]

Historical Materialism. The dialectical laws of matter produce different classes of beings and, at a certain point of evolution, also a thinking being, man. With the appearance of man history begins. History, as everything that is not primarily matter, is the product of matter. Consequently it is governed by the laws of dialectic. The application of the laws of dialectic to history produces the science of Historical Materialism.

History is shaped by individuals, as they are engaged in various relations in a given society. Marxist-Leninists distinguish two kinds of relations: economic relations and socio-ideological relations. The economic or material relations are called the *basis*, which is defined as "the economic structure of society, the sum-total of the production relations of the given society."[15] The socio-ideological relations are called the superstructure, which is defined as "the sum-total of social ideas, institutions and relations arising on the given economic basis." "The superstructure comprises three groups of social phenomena. First, social ideas, moods, social feelings, that is, ideology and social psychology. Second, various organizations and institutions—the state, courts, church, and so on. Third, superstructural (ideological) relations."[16]

The basis changes according to the development of the means of production from primitive to the sophisticated capitalistic form of production. Changes in the basis produce changes in the superstructure, which is therefore entirely determined by the economic formations. The social formations, that is, the social systems in which we live, are the result of the relations of production. It follows from this that history is ultimately determined by the "modes" of material production.

Marxist-Leninists claim that the dialectical laws of the basis and superstructure clearly prove that history is going inevitably toward perfect communism, which will be the fulfillment of all the potentialities and desires of man for a genuinely good and truly human life. First, *socialism* will be introduced by abolishing private ownership of all the means of production. Then, scientific socialism will organize production on a rational basis, eliminating the business cycles of capitalistic waste and depressions. It will build the industrial basis for the production of consumer goods and services. In this phase of history the motto is: "From each according to his ability, to each according to his work." The scientific organization of production, however, will slowly create such an abundance of goods and services that the era of *communism* will be ushered in. The motto of this phase of history is: "From each according to his ability, to each according to his needs." Money will be abolished and all the varied material and cultural needs of man will be satisfied without any payment. Since scarcity is the source of envy and all sorts of evil, abundance will change man's character, and his basic social traits of friendship, peace, mutual respect, orderliness and love will become dominant in individual and social relations. State power was introduced in history as a tool of oppression and a means to maintain some order. Since there will be no oppression in a communist society and the rational laws of social cooperation will be kept freely and voluntarily by the new type of man, there will not be any need for law enforcing agencies. As a consequence, the state will "wither away."

Marxism-Leninism states that throughout history morality was determined by the interests of the exploiting classes and imposed upon the oppressed to make them serve the ruling classes. Genuine Marxist morality of the present and of the future, however, is teleological and is determined by the necessary goal of

humanity, i.e., the fulfillment and liberation of man in
the perfect communist society. It follows from this that
the criterion of morality is human nature interpreted
according to Marxism-Leninism's philosophy of man.
Actions which are in accord with the ideal of perfect
communism or help the coming of the golden era
directly or indirectly are the morally good acts. Acts
which hinder the fulfillment of man in perfect communism and delay the coming of this culmination of
history are morally evil and criminal acts.

Evaluation. It is clear that the key to Marxist-
Leninist ethics is its theory of reality, i.e., the doctrine
of Dialectical and Historical Materialism. A thorough
critique of communist ethics, then, must be based on
the critique of Dialectical and Historical Materialism.
Here we can only indicate some problems critics of
Marxism-Leninism point out.[17]

The starting principle of Marxism-Leninism, that
all beings are either matter or products of matter, is not
proved but assumed and simply postulated. Modern
science offers many plausible, or at least puzzling,
theories indicating that the universe had an origin and
is not eternal. The basic question of why there is something and not nothing is never asked or answered.
Further, the "scientific" laws of dialectic are not accepted by science. Even communist scientists disregard them in their research.

As for Historical Materialism, the application of
the laws of dialectic to history do not work well and do
not prove the inevitable spread of communism all over
the world. Marxist-Leninists cannot satisfactorily
solve the contradiction between historical determinism and human freedom, which they defend. If
man is free and history is made by men, communism

as the ultimate goal of history is not inevitable. Man, in his freedom, can build other social systems than communism. The paradox of the communist thesis can be pointed out by asking the question: "Why should one organize a communist party and work hard to bring about a communism which will come anyhow by historical necessity?"

Economists have serious difficulty with the Marxist theory of future abundance of material goods and services. If the present is an indication, the Marxist-Leninist economic system has serious flaws and does not have the promise of future abundance.

The description of the golden era of history, in which all men will be good and cooperative as a result of a "redemption" by socialism and abundance, is so utopian that it cannot be taken seriously. The Soviet Union has officially reached socialism, and not yet the communist phase of development. According to impartial observers, however, the morally renewed man so far has not emerged there. The constant moral exhortations to honesty, sobriety and hard work on the part of the communist leadership are an indication that the hoped for "communist morality" is far from being in full bloom.

If man's ultimate end according to Marxist-Leninist philosophy is not realistic, its criterion of morality, too, becomes an empty phrase, without any objective content that might motivate a person's allegiance and commitment.

6. *Situation Ethics*

The postwar form of situation ethics is based on a certain type of existentialist philosophy notably represented by Jean-Paul Sartre. Existentialist philosophy is too complex and multifaced to be described in a few lines. The basic characteristic of existentialism is that it gives preference to the consideration of the dynamism of existence as against the understanding of a static essence or nature of man.

The type of existentialism represented by Sartre is atheistic. Essentialist philosophers, according to Sartre, speak about a great designer, God, who conceives the idea, the essence of man, and proceeds to make it existent by the act of creation. God's action is compared to a carpenter who, planning to make a desk, first designs the blueprint of the desk, and then proceeds to make it in his workshop. In this conception, essence precedes existence. According to Sartre, however, there is no God who would have designed the nature of man. Man is alone in this world without God. We are "trapped into existence"; the forces of nature brought us about without our consent. We do not first have a definite nature or essence. Our existence comes first, existence in freedom. What man makes of himself depends entirely on him and not on a given nature. There is no God to prescribe values. Man creates values in freedom and as he goes through life, he modifies these values according to the circumstances or the situation of human life. The morally correct act, then, is the one which is performed in freedom with due consideration of the actual situation.

One might think that the norm of existentialist ethics resembles that of moral positivism. It seems that an exterior, positive element, the changing situation, is the determining factor of morality. Some clarifications given by Sartre with regard to the "universal situation" of man, however, will modify this first impression. The universal situation of man is that he is necessarily in this world; he must work in order to live; he is necessarily among other human beings; and he is mortal. Freedom and this universal situation of man (as the norm for right conduct) can produce an order which is necessary for human living in this crowded world. In spite of this, however, Sartre insists that morality is entirely subjective. The necessary factors of human existence do not tell us what is objectively right or wrong. In addition, man has no purpose in life. Human life is meaningless, for as we build our existence through work and struggle and develop our personality, inevitable death finally comes to destroy everything. The philosophy of Sartre is pessimistic, and it is often called *the philosophy of the absurd*.

Evaluating the situation ethics of Sartre, one detects an inconsistency between his insistence on complete subjectivity in freedom, a kind of moral positivism, and his description of the "universal situation" of man. The latter seems to indicate that the necessity of some order in life forces Sartre to abandon his complete subjectivity and to accept some objective norm for the moral act. This objective norm appears to be the nature of man as he describes it, no matter how strongly he tries to reject the idea of human nature and the idea of its precedence over existence.

Joseph Fletcher's *Situation Ethics*, produced a lively controversy in the mid '60s in America but hardly any attention was paid to it in Europe. Fletcher calls the ethics of Sartre "antinomian," lawless ethics, and not situation ethics. He proposes his own system, which he considers to be a true situation ethics.

The situationist, according to Fletcher, accepts "the ethical maxims of his community and its heritage" and uses them as "illuminators of his problems."

But the situationist is ready "in any situation to com-
promise them or set them aside in the situation if love
seems better served by doing so."[18] It seems then, that
beyond the objective norms of the natural law and revelation, the most important and ultimately decisive
criterion of morality is love. Consequently, it is important to define clearly what love is. Fletcher tries to do
this by distinguishing three types of love: *Agapé* (giving love), *Philia* (friendship love), and *Eros* (romantic
love). "Agapé is giving love—non-reciprocal,
neighbor-regarding—'neighbor' meaning 'everybody,'
even our enemy. . . . It is usually distinguished from
friendship love (*philia*) and romantic love (*eros*) both
of which are selective and exclusive." The criterion of
the morally good act is agapé, although the two other
forms of love, too, "have their proper place in our
human affairs."[19]

Evaluation. The theory of Fletcher was mentioned here briefly, not because it is a well reasoned
and generally recognized philosophy, but because of
its emphasis on love. It may be very attractive to
stress the importance of love as the criterion of morality. It sounds alluring to state that the criterion of
morality is love and that our genuine moral obligation
is to act lovingly. But what does it mean for a person to
act lovingly?

According to the critics of Fletcher, one of the
great weaknesses of his ethics is that he never explains
in detail what love is. He gives some eleven different
roles to love in his *Situation Ethics*, and some of these
roles are clearly incompatible with others. Is the role
of love somehow determined by human nature? How
do we discover whether an act is done "lovingly" or
not? These are basic questions which are not answered
clearly by Fletcher.

VIII
Summary Consideration of the Norm of Morality

Ethical systems are distinguished from one another by the criterion of morality they explicitly or implicitly propose. Notwithstanding their professed differences, a careful analysis can point out a common element present in all of them. They are interested in the promotion of human well-being, making the life of man more "human," more satisfactory, more perfect and more complete. It seems that all ethicians have a certain idea of what man is and want us to live according to this idea of man. Their philosophy of man is not always explicit but it is the underlying basis upon which they build their ethical theories. Morality, then, seems to mean that man ought to be what he is by reason of his nature.

Even theories which base morality on extrinsic factors, as moral positivism does, are forced to fall back on some idea of man. They have to admit that legislation cannot be arbitrary since no society could survive if it disregarded the basic needs and aspirations of man given by his very nature. In other words, they have to take human nature into consideration as the basis of morally good or bad conduct.

The man in the street brands evil and cruel actions "inhuman," that is, contrary to human nature, and he speaks about humanizing man or bringing up his children as real human beings. One has to live according to human dignity, which is another term for human nature. Any legislation or action that harms our dignity or our humanity is called evil and inhuman.

What is the reason for this basic consensus regarding human nature as the criterion of morality, even if this consensus is sometimes expressed only implicitly while being contradicted explicitly? It seems that the ground for this consensus is the fact that, in its concrete application, we easily understand the abstract philosophical principle that "as a being is so it acts," i.e., that all beings have a nature, which is the source of their activities. All beings have goals built into their nature which they try to achieve. Man, of course, is a special being because his goals are not those of a plant or an irrational being. Through his intellect and will, man is an "open-ended" being. Nevertheless, we can discover natural, existential ends and drives in man which fit our nature and are demanded by it. There are natural existential goals which we cannot simply ignore. We have to exercise self-control in many of our natural activities such as eating or drinking; we have to overcome our irascibility, anger and despondency; we have to build habits that help us in our daily routines and enable us to lead a good human life. We have to live and work with others. We have to be born into a family and to be brought up and educated by others. We have to learn skills that will enable us to fit into society and live as human beings should live.

Non-free beings must act according to their nature by necessity. Man, being free, can go against his nature; he can act irrationally and antisocially. He should not do so, however, because going against his nature he degrades himself in his humanity. He becomes less of a human being. On the other hand, acting according to his naure, he builds his humanity, becomes more of a human being. Man is not born perfect and complete. He is not born morally good or bad but as he grows he realizes more or less the ideal of a perfect man as he performs acts which are in accord with his nature or are against it.

It seems, then, that most ethical systems regard human nature, at least tacitly and implicitly, as the criterion of morality, and it follows from our previous considerations that it is logical to state that the objective norm of morality is human nature.

It is important to have a correct understanding of the nature of man and not to take only one or another aspect of human nature as the norm. Man is spirit in matter. He is composed of body and spirit. This should not be understood as if we were put together, animality plus spirituality, as a sandwich of bread and ham is put together. To use an example, water is composed of hydrogen and oxygen, but this composition results in an entirely new being which is liquid and not gaseous. Man, as spirit in matter, is a new being, which is neither spirit nor matter, each part following the laws of its nature. Dualistic thinking about the nature of man could result in identifying morality with biological laws or with the laws of pure spirit or once with this, at another time with the other, without any consistency.

Human nature has to be understood completely, with all its constitutive elements—rationality, freedom, social character, relations of interdependence, man as planner, as self-manipulating and self-transcending being. Man's nature is dynamic, not static. He cannot be studied and analyzed as matter is analyzed in a laboratory. His nature cannot simply be taken apart and the parts of his nature scientifically listed once and for all. Man is a creative, self-transforming, self-transcending being. He can reach into his own nature through his intellect and his scientific creations. The question is whether this self-manipulation is wise or not, whether it increases his freedom and rationality, the fundamental characteristics of man, without which he would cease to be a human being. Man is dynamic also with regard to his end, as he constantly tries to transcend himself and never accepts the fact that he has realized all his potentialities. He refuses to admit that there is nothing more he could aim at. There is no limit to his aspirations. The infinite beckons him, as it were.

Although man can intervene in his own nature, nevertheless, he understands that he does not have unlimited power over his being. He does not even grasp the operations of his own nature, how his memory, his intellect and will work, how external stimuli are transformed into sensations of sound, light, odor, etc. In other words, man is a dependent being. He depends on many forces which he does not control, and he evidently did not make his own nature and the laws of his existence.

Agnostics and atheists will say that we depend on the blind forces of the universe. Believers in God, on the other hand, will explain the cause of our existence and the final goal of our life by pointing to a transcendent, rational and personal being upon whom all the forces of the universe depend. Our relation with this force is also part and parcel of our nature. One has rationally to choose one or the other understanding of the Force upon which we depend. We cannot always refer our actions to the ultimate reason of our existence, but in some cases a consideration of the ultimate foundation of our nature may be a decisive factor in determining the morality of an act.

The ultimate *force*, that is, the metaphysical foundation of our existence, is, at the same time, the *ultimate criterion of morality* because it is the reason why we are as we are. It is, however, not a practical and proximate criterion because we do not comprehend this force concretely and sufficiently.

Human Nature and History

Science measures the age of rocks and minerals and tells us that they have remained basically unchanged through billions of years. Living organisms, however, according to the theory of evolution, change and develop. Man is the end of the line of a long evolutionary process. Has this line of evolution been terminated so that modern man does not differ from primitive man? Or is the development of man's nature still going on? This question is important for ethics because changes in human nature would mean changes in morality too, if human nature is the criterion of the rightness or wrongness of human conduct.

Is the nature of primitive man identical with the nature of modern man? It is evident that both are human beings and that they are identical in this regard. Nevertheless, there is also a great difference between them. We can speak of an underlying identity, but we must also notice the great difference. This difference has to be taken into consideration when we use human nature as the measure of morality.

Human nature is dynamic. It is in man's nature, as Ignace Lepp wrote,[20] "to transcend continually or attempt to transcend his natural condition—not to free himself completely from nature but to acquire a new natural condition." As far as we know, man has not changed biologically since he became *Homo sapiens*. He has not grown wings to fly, but his intelligence has created jet airplanes and spaceships to fly faster than the birds. His hearing and sight have not become more acute, but his intelligence has produced the telephone, the radio and the television set, extending the range of his ears and eyes. His muscles have not become tougher and stronger, but machines have increased his strength a million times or more. Man illuminates the darkness of night and is not limited anymore by the changing of daylight and night. He heats and cools his dwellings, so he becomes free of the effects of the change of seasons. He has transformed his environment for better or worse and is affected by all the changes he has brought about. His intellect and free will are the cause of all these changes. These two fundamental constitutive elements of man, however, remain basically the same; without these, there is no man.

We have to understand that there are changes other than biological and physical. Correlations affect man and add something to his nature. The sum of the attributes of a man can change by his entering into relationships, for instance, by his getting married or becoming the president of a country. Although there is no physical change in these cases, the concrete and individual essence of man has been modified by these relationships, and the changed nature will determine the rightness or wrongness of many actions of a married couple or a president, like fidelity or infidelity in marital relations, or fulfillment of the responsibilities of the head of the government. A person who learns how to pilot an airplane or drive a car does not change; basically he remains the same. But the new skill affects his nature, so that the morality of his actions will also be affected. A skilled pilot may guide an airplane, while a person without this skill may not morally assume the responsibility of commanding an aircraft full of passengers. Man has changed a great deal since his appearance on this planet and all the changes affect his concrete nature in some way. Consequently, his nature, affected by the new relations, is the criterion of morality, and is the determining factor of his conduct.

But does not this constant change in human nature lead to a relativistic morality? It would, indeed, lead to relativism, if the changing elements were the only determining factors of morality. But, as John Macquarrie writes, "There are some constants which maintain themselves in the flux. To abandon static ideas of man and nature for more dynamic ones does not mean that notions of order and structure have been thrown away or that every culture and society, still less, every individual, is made sole author and arbiter of moral values."[21]

The dynamic idea of human nature means, however, that it is not like an electronic instrument that could measure morality with the precision of a laboratory test. We have to use prudent judgment and take into consideration many relationships that have affected the human condition throughout history. Most contemporary authors emphasize the historicity of human nature as the basic and unchanging attributes of nature are applied to the varying circumstances of a changing world.

It was mentioned earlier in this chapter that we

can discover existential goals in human nature. There are certain ends we have to attain in order to lead a human life. For instance, we have to achieve a certain degree of self-control and social cooperativeness; we have to acquire a great amount of knowledge through study to fit into a complex society and to survive in it. These partial existential goals indicate somehow the end of man whose achievement has to be promoted by actions which are in accord with human nature. Nevertheless, it would be difficult to find any person who could sincerely state that he has achieved the perfection of human nature, that he has arrived at the fullness of his humanity. But if we do not experience and concretely know the end of human nature, how can we use it as the measure of morality? We seem to be caught in a vicious circle.

The answer to this objection may lie in the fact that man is a dynamic reality, that he is "open-ended" in his goal and tries to transcend himself by his very nature. A house is completed when the last piece of brick is put in place according to the blueprint of the building. Even growing organisms like trees can reach the fullness of their potentialities, beyond which they cannot go. Man, however, is never completed in this sense. He is always capable of going beyond the degree of the perfection of the humanity he has already achieved. Nevertheless, we can somehow apprehend the goal towards which man strives with his characteristic activities. The true nature of man is revealed by those distinctive operations which enhance his humanity and thus take him closer to the completion of his potentialities. Consequently, even if we do not concretely see the completion of his potentialities, we can use man's nature as a measure of morality in as

much as we know what the distinctively human operation ... was aware of the self-transcending nature of man, and held that man cannot achieve his perfect ... happiness in this world. He proposed that
man can reach the fullness of his potentialities only
through a union with the infinite, that is, God, in the
beatific vision. Marxist Leninists speak of the "Absolute ... : ... all members of society will be
able ... develop all their talents and potentialities to the
fullest extent, and consequently will achieve happiness
living ... perfect society.

... human nature ... an impractical and extremely
complicated norm ... can hardly be known even by
experts. ... It seems that, in spite of the complexity of
human nature, we all know it fairly well in its major
operations. There is nothing closer to our consciousness than the ... operations of our nature, and
we ... ... cs, the principal drives and
tendencies of man by direct experience. This fact may
account for the fairly universal acceptance of the main
laws of moral living.

As human knowledge about reality has been increasing steadily from generation to generation, so
also is the understanding of the less clear and more
complex elements of man. Understanding the nature of
man is an ongoing process, and all the human sciences
contribute some clarification to our knowledge of what
the truly human is. Better knowledge of human nature
will enable us to judge the morality of complex problems which the development of science, especially biology, has introduced in our life in recent years.

IX
Comparing the Human Act with the Norm

Having established the criterion of morality, we have to develop a practical method by which we can compare a human act with the norm, in order to discern its morality. The application of the norm to a concrete case is not an exact laboratory test, for example, determining the chemical composition of an alloy. It is a fairly complex analysis that requires careful consideration and prudent judgment.

In order to facilitate this analysis, it is convenient to break down an act into its component elements and compare these elements, one by one, with the norm of morality. One has to be careful, however, not to separate the elements of an act in such a way as to lose the unity of the act and thus arrive at false conclusions.

It is customary to distinguish the following elements in a human act:

1. The object of the act, or what we do, for instance: helping a blind person across an intersection or taking money out of his pocket, telling a falsehood or telling the truth, volunteering for hospital work or going to a movie.

2. The motive of the act, i.e., the purpose that

prompts a person to act: telling a falsehood to get out of an embarrassment, or saving the life of a person who is sought by a maniac.

3. The circumstances, which answer the following questions: Who? Where? How much? How often? To whom? The person who performs an action, for instance, may be the president of a country or an ordinary citizen. These facts may influence the morality of his act. The president of a country should not play golf when urgent national problems have to be settled. The evil of theft may be increased by the amount one steals whether one steals the money from a destitute person or a wealthy corporation. One has to examine the circumstance carefully because not all circumstances influence the morality of an act. Some circumstances may be entirely irrelevant as far as the morality of an act is concerned.

4. The consequences or the effects of an act, strictly speaking, are not part of the act. Nevertheless, they are virtually contained in it in as much as they are caused by the act. These consequences can be foreseen or unforeseen. One takes a few drinks or smokes marijuana and, in spite of warnings of friends, drives one's car and gets into an accident. Or one is completely sober and, nevertheless, an accident happens. A union demands excessive wages and pensions and bankrupts a city, causing incalculable harm to all in that city. If union and city officials foresee the consequences, they are responsible for the bad effects of their action. In general, a person is responsible for foreseen consequences that follow directly from his act. He who wills the cause wills also the effect. We will discuss below the problem of multiple consequences which are partly good and partly bad.

In trying to decide upon the morality of an act, one has to see first whether the object, the motive and the circumstances of the act are in accord with the norm of morality, and then examine whether the effects of the act are harmful or beneficial.

The following diagram may help in this comparison. The object of the act may be good, indifferent or bad. The motive and circumstances also may be found good, indifferent or bad.

Object of act in itself:

Motive and circumstances:

An act which is good by its object becomes bad if the motive or circumstances are bad. For instance, giving somebody who is in financial difficulty a large amount of money with the intention of inducing him to vote for a bad and unjust law, makes an act of beneficence become an act of bribery.

An act which is indifferent by its nature may get its moral qualification from the motive or circumstances. Smoking a cigarette may be an indifferent act, but doing it to give a signal to criminals to hold up a bank becomes a bad act, and the person doing this becomes an accomplice.

Since an evil motive destroys the basic goodness of an act, one would be inclined to conclude that the reverse of this principle is also valid, that is, that a good intention or good end would change the evil character of an act. In other words, it could be asked whether a good end justifies an evil means or, as it is usually expressed in its abbreviated form, *whether the end justifies the means.* Is it right for Palestinian nationalists, intending to promote the liberation of their native land, to kill a number of athletes at the Olympics? Is it justified for exiled Croatians to skyjack an airplane in order to call the attention of the world to the violation of human rights in their native country?

The good intention is not enough to change the basic wrongness of an act because one must not consider the intention as a separate entity. One cannot will the end without willing the means and, if the means is bad by its very nature, one is already willing something that is wrong. A good intention is spoiled by the evil a person performs. If one element of the whole structure of the act is bad, the act cannot be said to be good. If you dial a phone number and miss it just by one digit, you still have a "wrong number."

Sometimes, however, it appears irrational not to choose the bad means to achieve a greater good. Is one obliged not to tell a falsehood in order to save the life of an innocent person who is sought by a maniac?

One of the solutions of this and similar cases can be found in the analysis of the means. Is the means, i.e., telling a falsehood really bad? The term "lie" already includes the concept that it is a morally wrong act. Can we distinguish the telling of a falsehood from lying, so that the expression of a falsehood would not be wrong in all cases? One has to be careful not to take the object of the act just in its physical reality. The object of an act can be very intricate. Attentive analysis will reveal its complexity. Human nature, taken as the norm of morality and applied to the problem of telling the truth leads us to the following consideration. Man is a social being. His physical, mental and spiritual needs are greater than his individual powers and they can be satisfied only through cooperation with other persons. We can conclude from this fact that mutual trust is a necessary aspect of human life because without it cooperation would be impossible. This means that we have to be truthful in our communication with others and that consequently all members of society have a right to the truth in general. Every right, however, can be limited by other rights and duties. A person using his right to truth not to help but to hurt others, abuses his right to truth and perverts the reason establishing this right. He consequently forfeits his right to this particular truth and need not be given a truthful answer. Telling a falsehood in this particular case would not go against human nature as the norm of morality. Misleading a maniac seeking someone's life would not be evil and should not even be called lying. This sort of analysis motivates many moralists to define lying as the denial of truth to a person who has a right to the truth. According to this definition, lying then, is not simply telling a falsehood with the intention to deceive, but has to be qualified as telling a falsehood to a person who has a right to the truth.

It has to be noted that in this case the good end does not justify the evil means because the means is not evil to begin with.

One could also appeal to the principle of *conflict of duties* to solve similar cases. When two duties, e.g., telling the truth and saving the life of an innocent person, are in conflict, the stronger and more important duty prevails or the lesser evil has to be chosen. This principle is based on the consideration that morality is the result of the agreement of an act with rational human nature. In other words, morality cannot impose contradictory duties upon us because it would be an irrational obligation. Recently the fear has been expressed by public officials that criminals might steal atomic devices or acquire the knowledge for making a crude atomic bomb and might then easily blackmail a whole city or nation. Suppose a criminal places an atomic device somewhere in Manhattan and notifies the mayor that the bomb will explode in five hours unless his demands are met. Suppose that this criminal is caught by the police but refuses to reveal the location of the bomb. May the police torture him to get the truth out of him? Two duties are in conflict here, the duty not to treat anybody in an inhuman way and the duty to save a city and possibly several million people. When two contradictory duties cannot be fulfilled, one has to choose the more important one and the other duty ceases to be a duty in the real sense of the term. Nevertheless, we have to be mindful that we have to try to solve the predicaments of real life by fulfilling both duties if it is possible at all.

The Principle of Double Effect

In the case of a foreseen evil consequence of an act, sometimes the *principle of double effect* may help us to decide whether we are allowed to perform the act or not. The rules of the principle of double effect have been developed by generations of moralists. They are based on the doctrine that we are not obliged to prevent the existence of all evil in the world. It is evident that we cannot wipe out all evil. Consequently we cannot be obliged to do it, since nobody can be obliged to do the impossible. The principle of double effect, however, goes further and explains and justifies the tolerance of some evil, even if it is the effect of our own deeds either because we cannot prevent it or because it would be unreasonably difficult to prevent it by not performing an act which is very important for our welfare.

"Double effect" means that an act has two foreseen consequences, one good and the other bad. The principle states that we are allowed to perform an act that has a bad effect under the following conditions:

1. The act we intend to perform is good or at least indifferent by its nature. Otherwise we would start on the wrong foot and would be doing something evil, which is forbidden by the moral law.

2. The good and bad effects follow simultaneously from the act, i.e., are caused independently by the act and the good is not the result of the evil. This latter would be against our previously established principle that the good end does not justify the evil means.

3. One only intends the good effect and merely tolerates the undesired bad effect. We are never allowed to will evil. Consequently, a person approving and intending the bad effect becomes directly involved in evil through the act of his will.

4. The good effect outweighs the bad effect, or at least there is a proportionately grave reason for permitting the evil effect. This proportion obviously cannot be easily measured and it takes careful analysis and prudent judgment to discern it.

The following diagram may be useful in the analysis of a case:

Right: [ACT] → good effect ⎫ ← proportion
            → bad effect ⎭

Wrong: [ACT] → bad effect ———→ good effect

An example: Several years ago when the Russians broke the moratorium on atmospheric atomic testing, a controversy arose in this country about whether the resumption of testing by the U.S. could be justified. It was argued that atmospheric testing contaminates the air by radiation and hence it would be immoral thus to endanger the lives of many human beings. On the other hand, others argued that an atomic explosion on a remote island is not bad by itself and the good consequences of the testing (i.e., the strengthening of the defenses of the country against Russian blackmail or attack) outweigh the bad effect of the increase of radiation. In addition, the good effect is not the result of the bad effect, that is, of the poisoning of the air, but follows directly and independently from the testing just as does the bad effect.

The principle of double effect finds a useful application in the moral analysis of *cooperation in evil*. One may be asked or forced to perform an act which in itself is not wrong but is used by others for their own evil purpose. For instance, gangsters may order a bank official to open a safe. Opening the safe in itself is not wrong, but it has two effects, one good and the other bad. If the official cooperates, one of the effects of his cooperation will be the saving of his life, which is good; the other effect will be bad, namely, the taking of the money from the bank. Were the bank official in collusion with the gangsters, he would actually intend the evil effect of his action and he would become a *formal* cooperator, which is forbidden by the rules of the principle of double effect. But, as is supposed, he does not intend the theft. He only tolerates it. Therefore, using the accepted technical term, he is a *material* cooperator. The good effect, that is, the saving of his life, outweighs the bad effect of the theft of money, and so he may open the safe without committing any moral evil himself.

Contemporary moralists caution us about the use of the principle of double effect. There is a danger, they warn us, in considering the two effects as independent entities while in real life the whole human act is one and unique. In addition, it is not always easy to separate the different elements of the act neatly and just tolerate the evil without really willing it.[22]

The warning is well placed and should make us careful in the application of this principle.

X
The Moral Law

The determination of the moral character of an act does not in itself impose upon us the obligation to perform or avoid an act. We may admit that we have to perform morally good acts *if* we want to be good persons, but this admission involves only a conditional obligation, a hypothetical necessity, and not an absolute duty, which Immanuel Kant called the *categorical imperative*. A person could say that he is not interested in being morally good and consequently does not feel bound to do the good.

Mankind, however, seems to be convinced that certain actions are absolutely forbidden, while others are unconditionally prescribed, and that it is not up to the individual to decide whether he wants to lead a morally good or bad life. It seems that people have some consciousness of a fundamental law that obliges us to do the good and avoid the evil. The fundamental law that comes before any enacted or positive law has been called, since ancient times, the *natural law*. Although the concept of the natural law has been expressed differently by various philosophers, a common element can be found in all descriptions, namely, that man has to live according to his true self and that all positive laws can be morally evaluated by comparing them with a fundamental justice based on the dignity of man's nature.

Is the belief in the existence of a moral law based on reality, or only on social conditioning, education and the clever manipulation of society by shrewd leaders?

The Concept of Law

Law in general means a necessity imposed upon a being to act in a certain way.

Physical law means acting in a certain way by physical necessity, e.g., the law of gravitation, kinetic energy and the laws of "nature" in general. As physical bodies, human beings are under the laws of nature and cannot defy them. If you hold your hand over a flame, it will get burned.

The moral law imposes moral necessity on free beings and obliges them to act in a certain way. Since moral necessity does not operate by physical force, we can go against the moral law, we can defy it. We may understand that we *should* not tell a lie, but we *can* tell lies.

What kind of force is moral necessity? What is the power behind the statement: "You ought to or ought not to do a certain thing?" There are two kinds of answers given to this question.

The Positivist Answer

Moral positivists affirm that the force of the moral law comes from the power of the government or of society to enforce the law. The moral force is basically the will of the lawgiver coupled with his power to impose the law on men who will comply with it because of the fear of punishment or of social ostracism. In other words, it is the "big stick" that gives effectiveness to the moral law.

The acceptance or rejection of this theory will depend on one's opinion concerning moral positivism. Independently of that, however, one may ask whether the fear of punishment is a sufficient motive or force to make people comply with the law. If there is no higher motive than fear for leading a decent life, then it seems a policeman would have to guard every person. How could 30,000 policemen keep the city of New York, with eight million people, in line? Moreover, the problem of making the law enforcing agencies themselves observe the law would remain unsolved. Who will guard the guardians?

It seems that people generally understand the importance of the goals to be achieved by certain laws and that it is this knowledge rather than the fear of punishment that prompts them to observe the moral laws of being honest, truthful, respectful of the property of others, etc. This leads us to the second theory concerning the nature of the necessity the moral law imposes upon us.

The Teleological Answer

Suppose I am in a forest and I want to reach a shelter before nightfall so that I will not be exposed to the cold and to danger from wild animals. Suppose, further, that I come to a crossroad and that one road is clearly marked as leading to the shelter and the other as leading away from it. It would be irrational not to take the road that leads to the shelter because I clearly understand the connection of the means, i.e., the road, with the end, i.e., the shelter, and I want to reach the goal, which is vital for me. Although I am not forced by physical power to take the road to the shelter, there is a moral necessity imposed upon me to take it.

The teleologists affirm that there are certain existential goals which are not of our own choosing, but are imposed upon us by our very nature. We can attain these goals only by performing certain acts. Hence the connection of an action with such a goal, that is, the relation of the means to the end, is the source of moral necessity. It is not as the result of our free choice that we are social and interdependent beings who have to cooperate with others. The necessary goals of social living can only be attained by certain cooperative acts. Furthermore, we are rational and free beings, not by our choice but by our very nature, and we have to act rationally and responsibly to comply with the existential drives and goals of our seeking truth and what is truly fulfilling of our nature.

The dynamic nature of man, seeking his own fulfillment, is the source of "oughtness." Man's nature is not simply a static fact but a tendency, a drive toward fulfillment. Man's nature is in process of achieving its fullness, the actualization of his potentialities. An act that promotes this process is not just a cold statistical event, but it is a link in the dynamic self-development of man toward the ideal of humanity.

The Natural Law Idea in History

The teleological answer we have described is basically the essence of the concept of the *natural law*. The idea that all laws come from God, or the gods, was prevalent in ancient cultures. Man lived under the forces of nature and all forces had a sacred character. Even human law was considered to have originated from God and to have been imposed upon men by the will of God. In primitive cultures, priests acted as judges, as an indication of the sacred and divine character of the law. In ancient Israel, according to the Book of Judges, the judges were priests.[23]

The idea of the natural law, as distinguished from humanly-enacted law, emerged in Greece. *Heraclitus* of Ephesus (ca. 536–470 B.C.) held that beyond the constantly changing phenomena there is a divine *logos* that keeps everything in harmony. "All human laws are nourished by this original divine law."[24] The metaphysical theories of *Plato* and *Aristotle* derive morality and moral obligation from the nature of man because the fulfillment of the nature or essence of man is at the same time his goal which he has to attain. Although Aristotle did not use the term, *natural law*, many medieval philosophers considered him as one of the first and most systematic exponents of the fundamentals of natural law. *Stoicism*, a philosophy founded by *Zeno* (ca. 340–265 B.C.), was the first to introduce the term, *natural law*. (Stoicism is named after "stoa," a portico, where Zeno taught.) Stoic philosophy spanned several centuries and greatly influenced *Cicero* (106–43 B.C.) and many prominent Roman lawyers, writers and statesmen. This philosophy integrated many elements of the best Greek tradition in philosophy. Its theory of virtue is an application of the natural law idea. Virtue is firm and unwaivering conduct in agreement with man's rational nature. There is a universal law governing the whole world, and the wise man willingly obeys this eternal world law as it is manifested through his rational nature.

Cicero was a strong advocate of the natural law idea as it was proposed by stoicism. He spoke eloquently of an innate, unchangeable law which is the basis of all positive laws. We quote here one of his better known statements on this subject:

If the principles of Justice were founded on
the decrees of peoples, the edicts of princes,
or the decisions of judges, then Justice would
sanction robbery and adultery and forgery of
wills, in case these acts were approved by the
votes or decrees of the populace. But if so
great a power belongs to the decisions and
decrees of fools that the laws of Nature can
be changed by their votes, then why do they
not ordain that what is bad and baneful shall
be considered good and salutary? Or, if a law
can make Justice out of Injustice, can it not
also make good out of bad? But in fact we can
perceive the difference between good laws
and bad by referring them to no other standard, than Nature: indeed it is not merely Justice and Injustice which are distinguished by
Nature, but also and without exception things
which are honorable and dishonorable. For
since an intelligence common to us all makes
things known to us and formulates them in
our minds, honorable actions are ascribed by
us to virtue, and dishonorable actions to
vice; and only a madman would conclude that
these judgments are matter of opinion, and
not fixed by Nature.[25]

St. Augustine (354–430), emphasized the source
of the natural law which, in his opinion, is the *eternal
law*. God governs the world by his eternal law, which
has been in the mind and will of God from all eternity.
The world and man participate in this eternal law when
they become existent through God's creative act and
begin to function according to the laws of God. The

natural moral law is the rational creature's participation in the eternal law of God. *St. Thomas Aquinas* and the great Scholastic philosophers and theologians defended and refined the ideas of both the eternal law and the natural law. The doctrine of the natural law became firmly established in the Middle Ages and was fairly universally accepted until about the middle of the 18th century.

The turning away from the natural law in that era was a reaction to the exaggerated insistence of rationalism on the power of human reason. Some philosophers of that time maintained that we can prove all the precepts of the natural law in a mathematical way, right down to the smallest detail. Such an extreme position discredited the idea of the natural law as a guiding principle. (It has to be applied prudently to the varying circumstances of human life and not be taken as a detailed statutory law.) Utilitarianism and positivism rejected natural law as a source of moral obligation and, instead, emphasized utility, the positive law, societal pressure and public opinion as the sources of obligation. Legal positivism in individual and international affairs became widely accepted by jurisprudence. Nevertheless, the idea of the natural law did not die out completely.

The decades after World War II have experienced a revival of the doctrine of the natural law even if the doctrine has not always been expressed under the name of natural law. The principles of the natural law, however, are being proclaimed more and more explicitly. *The Charter of Human Rights*, adopted by the United Nations in 1948, gives a list of human rights which are based on the nature of man and have an undeniable validity before any positive law. The many

reform or revolutionary movements of the postwar
period usually appeal to a higher law and a fundamental justice which have to be obeyed and respected before any positive law of governments.

The Nuremberg trial of war criminals in 1945
prompted an interesting discussion of the natural law
doctrine.[26] The basic legal principle, "no punishment
where there is no law," was brought up by defense
lawyers in favor of those accused of war crimes. It was
pointed out that some of the laws the war criminals
allegedly violated, were only enacted after the alleged
violations had uccurred, so that they were not in force
at the time of the alleged crimes. The prosecution,
however, argued that those laws have always been in
force and that positive enactment did not create the
obligation to observe them, but only gave expression
to this obligation in writing. Justice Robert H.
Jackson, the Chief Counsel for the United States, argued that there are some basic laws of humanity which
are valid before any positive enactment. Even if there
is no positive law against genocide and the liquidation
of the "unfit," these acts are crimes against humanity,
and the persons committing them are guilty. M. Fran-
cois de Menthon, Chief Prosecutor of the French Republic, expressed the same conviction: "There can be
no well-balanced and enduring nation without a common consent in the essential rules of social living,
without a general standard of behavior before the
claims of conscience, without the adherence of all citizens to identical concepts of good and evil."[27]

The attention of world public opinion has been
focused in recent years on the mistreatment of "dissi-
dents" in various countries. Many statements are
made, and articles and books are written in defense of

their rights, which are based on the "dignity" of man, that is, on the nature of man. These are rights guaranteed by the natural law. On March 18, 1977, in his address at the United Nations, President Carter exhibited the same conviction when he said: "The search for peace and justice means also respect for human dignity. . . . The basic thrust of human affairs points toward a more universal demand for fundamental human rights."[28]

Although the term, "natural law," is not used frequently these days, there is every indication that the idea itself is very alive and that the validity of the natural law is recognized more and more all around the world.

XI
Finding the Moral Law in Human Nature

If the natural law is basically identical with the dynamic nature of man as the source of his activities, an analysis of human nature should find it there. The natural law is a moral necessity imposed upon a person by his nature to do the true good and avoid the real evil. Since we are looking for the laws of human nature as it is distinguished from other natures, we should be able to locate this moral necessity in those faculties by which man specifically differs from inorganic, organic and animal natures. These specific faculties of man are his intellect and will. Consequently, we should find the necessity of the moral law in the functioning of these faculties.

As for the operation of the *intellect*, we find that it deals with truth. When I state that the whole is greater than one of its parts, that is, when a truth is clearly presented to me, my intellect must assent to it. In other words, truth necessitates the intellect. Truth, of course, is not always transparent and evident, but it may consist of a chain of complicated statements and deductions. In such cases our intellect will not be forced to assent until we see the evidence.

A similar necessity is found also in the functioning of our *will*. We cannot will something unless there is some good in that object. This good may be only an apparent good, but the will cannot move unless it is attracted by someting desirable in the object. The desirable element of the action somehow fits into a person's judgment on the progress of man toward his fulfillment even if this is only a very limited advance. For instance, a person committing suicide finds some good in it, possibly liberation from a painful disease, shame, emptiness of life or some other reason. Our conclusion is that the good in general, i.e., the desirable, necessitates the will.

This description of the functioning of our intellect and will may seem to prove that we are determined in our actions, that the necessity we have found is more than moral necessity. In a certain sense it is true that we are determined always to choose under the aspect of good. We can admit that we are not free in this regard. Our freedom consists in the fact that we can consider a great number of acts and objects, in almost all of which we can find something attractive which we can deliberately choose. If an object appeared to be absolutely bad, we could not act. Some persons develop abnormal obsessions and consequently suffer a certain limitation of their freedom because everything looks bad and frightening in objects. Psychologists who deal with these strange cases of loss of freedom, try to convince their patients that the objects of their obsession are not bad and harmful so that their paralysis may disappear.

Since our intellect and will are not two independent entities in us; but the faculties of a person who, through them, seeks truth and goodness, we can state that there is a fundamental law in our nature that obliges us to do the true good and avoid the real evil. This obligation, however, does not amount to a physical necessity because, under normal conditions, we are free to choose among various goods. Nevertheless, this necessity is a real moral force found in our nature, because we understand that we are bound to choose the true good and avoid the real by virtue of the operations and tendencies of our principal faculties.

The Positive Law

Truth is grasped by our intellect when it is clearly presented. The major existential goals of man are experienced by every normal man and easily apprehended as the sources of moral obligations. The more complex facts, goals and relationships of our nature, however, are not easily perceived and so the duties arising from them are not accepted by everybody. Consequently, the natural law, which is basically identified with human nature, cannot direct us in the detailed and complex problems of life. Nevertheless, it remains the source of obligation because it has to be applied to the various and ever changing problems of human life through the mechanism of the *positive law*.

Every organized society enacts positive laws which, in some sense, are the applications of the natural law and therefore may not contradict its principles or violate the rights of man which are derived from it. A general principle of the natural law obliges us to cooperate with one another in building a society and promoting the common good. This command of the natural law follows clearly from the existence of human needs which are greater than our individual powers can provide for and that can be satisfied only through cooperation with our fellow men. The precept is clear in its general direction but it does not tell us what the detailed rules of cooperation should be; these are not inscribed in our nature. These rules will depend on the actual situation and have to be decided by prudent positive laws. Hence we can conclude that the natural law obliges us to obey the just laws of legitimate authority. One can easily understand, for instance, that there must be order in transportation, but the detailed traffic laws which achieve this order have to be decided by positive legislation since there is no indication in our nature about which side of the road we should drive on. In some cases there may be two or more equally good ways to achieve a certain societal goal but only one of them can be chosen to avoid chaos in social cooperation. In this case, too, positive legislation has to decide which one of the ways has to be followed by everybody.

The existence of the natural law, then, does not make positive laws superfluous; on the contrary, it grounds them in reality and keeps them within the bounds of justice. Any positive law which contradicts the natural law loses its validity because its obligatory force is derived from the natural law.

The Mutability and Immutability of the Natural Law

The mutability and immutability of the natural law is a problem that caught the interest of its advocates from the very beginning of the emergence of the idea of natural law. If the natural law is changeable, morality becomes relative. If, on the other hand, the natural law is unchangeable, it gets too rigid to serve as a credible guiding principle in a constantly changing world.

As we have discussed earlier, human nature is

dynamic and is in constant progress toward the achievement of the ideal of human nature. This fact would account for the evolution of moral consciousness in history and an apparent mutability of the natural law. At the same time there are permanent elements in man's nature which give constancy to the moral law and eliminate the danger of relativism. As a child grows up, his relationship to his parents changes; at a certain age he will be emancipated from the authority of his parents and no longer will owe the same obedience to them as before. The duty of his parents toward him will change, too; they will not have to support him any more. Man has been growing from infancy to a more mature existence throughout history. His knowledge of reality has increased tremendously. He has changed his environment and, in the process, he has been affected by all the changes. Just as the duties and rights of an adult differ from those of a child, the duties and rights of the members of an industrial society differ from the duties and rights of an agricultural or primitive community. The meaning of responsible parenthood has undergone changes, now that the human race is not threatened by extinction but rather, by rapid growth.

Such an evolution of man is furthered by his very nature. It is due especially, to his reason. The ignorance of primitive man was overcome through the reasoning power of generations who have built civilizations and cultures. The changing of man and, consequently, the mutability of the natural law in this sense, is consistent with nature. St. Thomas recognized such an evolution as man progressed from an imperfect state to a more perfect one.[29] At the same time, one could insist that no real changes have taken place in the natural law; only the circumstances have changed, and the unchangeable natural law indicates what morality is under the new circumstances. Furthermore, man learns more and more about his own nature and consequently the application of the natural law to the human condition becomes more refined and better understood.

There is no need to sharpen the opposition between these two positions. The basic characteristics of man are not changeable. We will never become animals. Thus we have to live with the "honor and burden" of being rational, free, responsible beings. On the other hand, man has definitely been affected by the intellectual and cultural evolution mankind has travelled through from the dawn of history until our present time. Cultural and intellectual evolution will be reflected in moral consciousness and in the moral judgment man forms about his evolving condition. We could conclude that the natural law is as changeable and unchangeable as human nature is changeable and unchangeable.

Knowledge of the Natural Law

The natural law is not a statutory law, i.e., it is not found clearly expressed in legal codes; it is not promulgated by a government in official publications. How do we learn, then, about the duties imposed upon us by the natural law? If we do not know of the existence of a law, we cannot be bound by it because the moral law does not obtain compliance by physical force but through the conscious and free cooperation of rational beings.

The natural law is dynamic human nature as it is directed toward its own completion through conscious and deliberate actions. The knowledge of the natural law, then, will depend on our ability to know our own nature. Human nature is a complex reality, and we do not know all the details and all the references of our nature. On the other hand, we have a direct experience of our nature. It is actually closer to us than anything else. All normally developed persons understand the major necessary existential goals of man and the means that lead to these ends. In other words, we do know and understand the major precepts of the natural law by reflecting on the existential ends of man and the means that lead to them. As we grow up and face the challenges of life, we naturally recognize the major rules of decent human living.

What, concretely, are the precepts which normally developed persons recognize? The fundamental principle is that good has to be done and evil has to be avoided. This basic and primary principle is easily applied to the major problems man faces in his life, and the consequences are drawn without much difficulty. Moralists used to identify the evident precepts of the natural law with the second table of the decalogue, i.e., respect and obedience toward parents, obedience toward lawful authority, respect for the life and bodily integrity of our fellow men, faithfulness in marriage, truthfulness in our communication with others, respect for the rightful property of others, keeping of agreements and promises. This does not mean that sometimes people do not err in the application of the natural law even in these self-evident cases. More involved aspects of human nature need to be studied more carefully, and sometimes even a prolonged and sophisticated research cannot dispel all ambiguity. The human mind does not have compartments for the various fields of reality, e.g., one compartment for mathematical truths, another for historical facts and another for moral truths. We have one intellect that tries to understand reality no matter what the nature of that reality is. Simple truths, for instance, twice two is four, seem evident even for children. More complex truths, e.g., the rules of differential calculus, are not easily grasped even by educated persons because they are involved and do not appear evident without reflection and study. In the field of morality, too, some facts are evident, while others are more intricate and are not easily apprehended by everybody. New developments in molecular biology raise difficult moral problems because not all the facts and not many of the consequences of certain biological interventions are known even by the experts. It is natural that moral judgments in these cases may be hesitant and sometimes quite mistaken. Errors will be sometimes discovered only after more research clarifies the facts involved in these cases. We do not know much about the results and consequences of gene-splicing, for example. Consequently, our moral judgment on this type of genetic engineering will be hesitant or hypothetical.

Science and the humanities have greatly contributed to our knowledge of reality. They continue to discover more and more truths about our existence and the relationships of our nature to the world. This means further progress in the knowledge of morality, too. The natural law, then, is known and promulgated to us through our reason as we understand the reality of man and what it means to build a truly human life.

Sanction of the Natural Law

A positive law is not considered really a law unless it has sanctions attached to it. A positive law without sanction is taken for a recommendation, as advice that does not impose an obligation upon us. Sanction is a penalty attached to the violation of a law, by means of which authority enforces the law. The penalty can be a fine, jail, the loss of some advantage or any other form of punishment. Is there any sanction attached to the natural law? Obviously, there is no positive sanction connected with it, although the natural law may be frequently enacted as a positive law with a proper sanction attached to it. Examples are the positive laws forbidding murder, theft and perjury, which in all countries have proper sanctions attached to them.

Nevertheless, we can speak of the sanction of the natural law in a certain sense. Compliance with the natural law signifies actions that take us closer to the fulfillment of our nature and the reaching of our existential goals. If we are not using the means to reach our natural existential goals, but on the contrary, perform actions which move us away from those goals, we suffer a penalty, a loss of our humanity. We become less "human," in the sense that we are getting away from the ideal of humanity.

The violation of the natural law always disturbs the social order and makes life less orderly and less human even for the person who offends the natural order. History is a witness that small or large communities suffer a great deal when a significant number of people violate the natural law. Fear spreads in the cities, mutual suspicion pervades the atmosphere, business moves out, unemployment grows, and so on. On the national level, when people are deprived of their basic rights, are exploited, when social justice is violated, when a government abuses its power, the consequences of all these transgressions of the natural law are tension, loss of harmonious and orderly living, violence and many other penalties, which are all rather severe sanctions for the breaking of the natural law. Disregarding the natural law in international relations brings with it equally severe consequences, as history bears witness. The natural law, then, has real sanctions and these sanctions ensue from the essence of the natural law. They mean the missing of the existential goals of the individual and of communities.

XII
Rights

Human Rights

The recognition of moral obligation is a common experience of mankind. Nobody can sincerely claim that he has never encountered the force of the moral law in his conscience. We further experience a moral force in the execution of our duty that empowers us to use the appropriate means by which we can fulfill our obligation. It seems contradictory to us to be obliged to do something and not to be given the means for the fulfillment of the duty. It logically follows from the existence of duty that the person upon whom the duty is imposed must have a justified claim to the appropriate means for the carrying out of his duty and also a claim to restrain others from interfering with his action in the line of duty. We take it as self-evident that if we are hired to perform a certain work, we must be given the appropriate tools or means for that job. If somebody is hired as a mechanic, a tailor or printer, he has to be given the materials and tools for his work.

Moral duty entails a claim to the appropriate means and freedom of action to fulfill the duty. This claim is called *right*. Since rights are correlatives of moral duties, they share the characteristics of moral duty. It follows, then, that as an obligation imposes a moral and not a physical necessity upon us, a right gives us moral power and not physical force, to have the means necessary for the fulfillment of our duty.

Right can be defined as the moral power to have what is justly due to a person, or the moral power to claim, do, omit or possess something free from interference by others. Right, as moral power, works by appeal to the intellect and will of another person who should respect our right.

Rights are based on law and are logically derived from duties imposed upon us by law. Different ethical systems have different understandings of the essence of right according to their respective interpretations of moral obligation. If the will of the government is the source of moral obligation or morality is based on public opinion and consensus, as the moral positivists hold, then all rights are granted to us by the government or society and there are no rights other than those. If, however, there exists a fundamental moral law that precedes the will of the government or society, there also exist fundamental rights which are independent of the command of the government and are not granted to the citizens by social authority. Rather, the government and society are obliged to respect and defend these antecedent rights.

The structure of rights. A right is based on law, and its essence is a claim to certain things. This means that in every right we can distinguish a number of relations. According to accepted terminology, the following four elements are found in every right: the subject, the term, the object and the title of right.[30]

1. The subject of a right is a person who has the claim to something.

2. The term of a right is another person who is obliged to respect the right or satisfy the claim.

3. The object of a right is a thing to which a person has a claim.

4. The title of a right is the reason that justifies the claim of a person to the object of a right.

The following diagram may help us to understand the relations of these four elements in the structure of right:

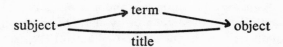

Rights are involved in many aspects of our daily life. When you buy a new car, you acquire a right to that car; you have a legitimate claim to its ownership. In the transaction, you become the subject of a right; the salesman is the term of the right, because he has to fulfill your claim to the car; the car is the object of your right, and the money paid is the title upon which your right is grounded.

The subject and term of a right can only be persons either physical or corporate. This follows from the essence of law and the essence of right. Only rational beings can be bound by moral law and can respect the rights of others. Animals, then, do not have rights. Nevertheless, we are bound by morality to treat animals according to our rational nature and not in an irrational and cruel manner.

The objects of a right can be material things like land, a house, an oil well—or immaterial things, like the idea of an invention. Man may have full control over material or immaterial things, but he may never have unrestricted power over another person. A person may never be an object of a right because a person may not be used as a means for others since every person has his own goal and is master of his own destiny. Slavery, which treats human beings as mere things, contradicts the very essence of right. We may have a right to the services of other persons so long as these services do not contradict their existential ends as human beings. No contract can be valid that would oblige a person to perform services which are immoral. As Messner writes: ". . . any labor contract . . . includes an implicit clause providing that the worker's human person and its existential responsibilities will be respected; it is therefore a deviation from the natural order of law if an economic system . . . imposes working conditions that prevent men from fulfilling their duties toward their families, whether by underpayment or by reckless exploitation of their powers."[31]

The title of a right is the foundation that supports the subject's claim to the object of that right. If the title is an accidental fact not belonging to the essence of a person, such as the purchase of a house, the right involved is called *acquired right*. If the title is an essential element of human nature and existence, the resulting rights are called *congenital or natural rights*. Recently, the term *human rights* is used more and more for the idea of natural rights.

It is also customary to speak of inalienable rights. The usual understanding of the term is that nobody can take these rights away from a person since they are not granted to him by society or any human authority. Strictly speaking, however, inalienable rights are those human rights a person himself may not give up, even voluntarily, because they are absolutely necessary for a moral life. For instance, we may not give up the right to live according to our honest conviction, that is, renounce the right to follow our conscience.

Alienable rights are those human rights which we are allowed to give up. For instance, every competent adult has the right to get married, but a person may give up his right to marry provided he is not forced to do it.

Natural Rights, Human Rights

In the previous chapter we considered the existence of a natural or fundamental law that precedes any positive law. No positive law may conflict with the precepts of the natural law. If a positive law is enacted which is contrary to the natural law, it is an invalid and unjust law that must not be obeyed.

The existence of natural rights logically follows from the existence of the natural law. If we are bound to perform certain actions because of our nature, we also have the natural claim to the means by which we can fulfill our obligation or, in other words, we have natural rights.

The doctrine of natural rights goes back to ancient Greece and possibly even earlier times. It is well known from history, however, that natural rights have not always been respected. Many political systems violated the natural rights of their citizens. On the other hand, many countries, including the United States, owe their existence to the claim to independence based on natural rights or, as the Declaration of Independence calls them, "certain inalienable rights."

History has recorded the struggle of many peoples for the recognition of the natural rights of citizens against oppressive governments or conquering powers. Although great progress has been made in this regard since ancient times, the protection of human rights is very uneven, to say the least, even in our times. There are governments that deliberately and systematically violate and limit the natural rights of their citizens. This happens in spite of the fact that on December 10, 1948, the General Assembly of the United Nations adopted the Universal Declaration of Human Rights or, as it is frequently called, the *Charter of Human Rights*. The General Assembly proclaimed this Universal Declaration of Human Rights "as a common standard of achievement for all peoples and all nations." The Charter intends to strengthen respect for basic human rights because "disregard and contempt for human rights" are criminal acts and destroy the foundation for harmonious and decent human living. The Charter has 30 articles and lists a great number of rights, most of them based on the nature and existence of man. In articles 18 and 19, for instance, it mentions freedom of conscience:

> Everyone has the right to freedom of thought, conscience, and religion; this right includes freedom to change his religion or belief, and freedom either alone or in community with others and in public or private, to manifest his religion or belief in teaching, practice, worship, and observance.
>
> Everyone has the right to freedom of opinion and expression, this right includes freedom to hold opinions without interference and to seek, receive, and impart information and ideas through any media and regardless of frontiers.

Since the Charter does not have the force of law, sixteen European nations decided to strengthen the

defense of human rights by an enforceable international law and ratified the European Convention on
Human Rights on September 3, 1953. The Convention
gives individuals as well as governments the right to
petition the international organization and go to the
international court to redress grievances.

Might Is Not Right

A right appeals to the intellect and will of another
person to respect it. In other words, right is not
grounded in physical force but in moral power. It follows from this that the claim to the means for the fulfillment of a person's existential ends remains valid
even if a stronger person takes them away. Rights are
not derived from physical power and the stronger may
not justly dominate the weaker. This essential trait of
right is expressed in the dictum: "*might is not right.*"

Right cannot be equated with might but we are
allowed to use physical force to defend our rights.
Since isolated individuals usually are too weak to defend their rights, they are naturally inclined to form
societies. One of the primary goals of society is the
adequate defense of the rights of the individuals
through a legal order which can be maintained by a
proper organization and even by the use of force if it
becomes necessary.

Since the legally organized society has assumed
the task of defending individual rights, it would be
wrong for an individual to resort to force in safeguard-
ing his rights unless there is an emergency at a time
when the proper authority cannot intervene, as in the
case of self-defense against imminent aggression.
When a society does not adequately assure the safe
possession of individual rights because the authorities
are negligent, corrupt or inept, it becomes inevitable

that individuals will resort to force in the defense of their legitimate rights. They will organize groups of vigilantes or other organs of self-defense. Such a state of affairs is a sign of very serious defects in the political body, which may lead to chaos and the disintegration of a society.

Rights to material objects can be enforced by the use of physical power or in the courts. For instance, one can regain stolen property when the police arrest the thief. These rights are called juridical rights. There are rights which cannot be physically enforced, e.g., the parents' right to the love of their children. These rights are called non-juridical rights. The existence of non-juridical rights indicates again that right cannot be identified with might, with physical force.

Limitation of Rights

Life in society is based on mutual respect of rights. This means that rights are limited by their very nature, as they come into conflict with the rights of others. Freedom of speech does not entitle a person falsely to shout "fire" in a crowded theater, because others have the right not to be deceived, not to be exposed to danger by a false alarm and not to be disturbed in their enjoyment of a play. It follows from this that freedom of speech has a number of limitations. Every right is limited by the duties which are in conflict with it.

A right is limited also by its purpose, by the end it serves. It does not grant moral power to a person beyond the goal of a right because a right is a means to achieve a particular end. Everybody has the right to freedom of religion and to the belief that his own religion is the true one, but this freedom does not empower a person to force others to accept his religion. The purpose of the right of freedom of religion is to permit a person to follow his own conscience in religious matters without interference, but the moral power to do this does not extend to forcing others to join his religion.[32]

XIII
The Moral Judgment—
Conscience

Having established the standard of morality, a person will, as a logical step, apply this criterion to concrete problems as he faces moral decisions day after day. The application of the norm or criterion of morality results in a moral judgment that determines the rightness or wrongness of an action to be performed. It further declares whether an action is obligatory, permitted, or has to be avoided.

The intellect formulating a moral judgment is called conscience. There is, however, some confusion about the meaning of conscience in the minds of many persons. Since most people are indoctrinated as to the morality of certain actions by their parents, the school system, their church, public opinion or a combination of all these, the formation of a moral judgment comes very quickly and easily, almost without reflection. This fact has induced some philosophers and certainly many a man in the street to conclude that conscience is some mysterious entity in us, some special faculty of the intellect that works automatically, or that it is the "voice of God" in us, that tries to keep us on the right path.

A careful analysis, however, reveals that conscience is a judgment of our intellect on the rightness or wrongness of an action. We use phrases like "my conscience tells me," "my conscience forbids me," etc., and the popular mind imperceptibly invests this "voice of conscience" with the characteristics of an almost independent being in us. But examining the "voice of conscience" we find that there is nothing really mysterious about it. It is only a quick application to concrete cases of some ethical principles we have learned and accepted in childhood or in later years.

These ethical principles are readily available in our mind and are applied, through a quick deductive process of reasoning, to the problem we actually face. We have learned and accepted, for instance, the principle that stealing is wrong, and encountering a situation in a store where we could easily pocket an article, we reason quickly, "our conscience tells us," that shoplifting is stealing and consequently wrong and that we should not do it.

The ethical principles we follow are the result of inductive reasoning and, as such, they may change when new evidence is adduced, a previous argument is refuted or an authority is rejected. Sometimes we may arrive at a conclusion that the principles are not universally valid. The judgment then will be about the problem of whether the case in question is an exception. In general, however, we form principles which we hold as universally valid. Their application, therefore, is carried out in a deductive way, that is, we follow the rules of the syllogism. In every syllogism there is a "major" statement, which is compared with the "minor," from both of which, then, the conclusion is deduced. For instance, theft is wrong (major), and taking this jewelry is theft (minor); consequently, taking this jewelry is wrong. The application of the principle does not always occur explicitly. It can happen in a very quick, cursory manner, without even mentioning the principle. Nevertheless, the moral principle we have previously established or accepted is the basis for the judgment of conscience.

It is obvious that the correctness of the principles in any deductive reasoning of our conscience is the main factor in arriving at a correct moral judgment, for if the principles are wrong, the consequences also will be wrong. As we mature and deliberately reflect on the moral principles we learned in our childhood, we have to examine whether those principles are correct or erroneous. We may find that we have gradually assimilated prejudices from our social milieu, the school or the family. It follows, then, that we have to overcome our prejudices and correct our thinking so that our principles will coincide with truth. Growing up means examining all our moral principles, modifying those which are false and accepting the true ones on the basis of our own rational conviction, and not on the basis of the authority of others.

The process of examining our moral principles is ultimately nothing else but the application of the norm of morality to the concrete problems of human life. In this way one rationally builds a body of moral rules which are readily available and are easily applicable to particular cases when one has to make a moral decision. This body of moral rules will eliminate the necessity of constantly going back to the fundamental norm of morality, which would make the moral decision cumbersome in everyday situations. This procedure is called "forming one's conscience." If all the reasoning involved is done correctly, one has a "well formed conscience." The task of moral education is to form one's conscience on a rational basis so that one can make correct moral decisions through his own conviction.

Correctness of the Judgment of Conscience

As we examine the functioning of conscience, it is important to be acquainted with some concepts dealing with its operations.

Correct conscience. The moral judgment of our intellect is correct when all the reasoning involved in the application of the objective norm of morality is carried out logically and without any mistake.

Erroneous conscience. The judgment of conscience is erroneous when it is based on false principles or applies the correct principles in a faulty way, consequently falsely declaring an action to be good or evil.

An erroneous conscience can be *invincibly* erroneous when we cannot overcome the error by means which are at our disposal or which we can prudently procure.

Conscience is *vincibly* erroneous when the error can be overcome and the false judgment can be corrected.

Certainty of the Judgment of Conscience

A *certain conscience* means that the person making the moral judgment has no reasonable ground to doubt the correctness of his judgment.

A *doubtful conscience*, on the other hand, means that the person making the judgment has a reasonable ground to fear that the opposite of his judgment may be true.

It follows from the previous definitions that both

the correct and the erroneous conscience can be either certain or doubtful.

Certitude and correctness are not the same thing. It may happen that we are entirely convinced of the reality of some happening, for instance, in sports, and yet we discover later, when the event is replayed in slow motion on television, that we were mistaken. Five witnesses may describe an accident in five different ways, all of them convinced that they are telling the truth.

It is important to note that a doubt may be based on the obscurity of a fact or on the obscurity of a law in question. The time-honored example is the case of the hunter who is not certain whether the object that moves is a deer or a man. This uncertainty is called *a doubt of fact*. If the hunter is not certain whether the law forbids the shooting of deer in that particular season, we have a doubt of law or doubt of obligation. In the first case there is no doubt about the obligation or the existence of the law forbidding one to shoot a human being, while in the second case the doubt is about the existence of the obligation not to shoot deer.

The Rules of Conscience

The rules of conscience are not arbitrary impositions upon our moral freedom; they are deduced from the nature of man and from the structure of a conscious and deliberate human act.

1. The *first* rule obliges us always to obey a certain conscience.

a. A correct and certain conscience is an unconditional norm of human conduct. One has to obey it when it prescribes or forbids an action.

b. An invincibly erroneous and certain con-

science is a conditional norm of human conduct. It is
valid only on the condition that the person has done his
best to find the truth and draws an erroneous conclusion through no fault of his own.

One has to obey the invincibly erroneous, certain
conscience because the human way to act is to follow
the light of one's reason. Otherwise a person would go
against his nature. It is a part of the human condition
that our intellect is a finite means to finding truth and
this means that we can make errors in our reasoning.

The certitude which is required need not be
greater than an assurance gained by a prudent investigation and reflection. No one can be obliged to do
more than his human condition can achieve.

2. The *second* rule forbids us to act with a doubtful conscience. The reason for this rule is that it is
possible that in case of doubt we shall be doing something objectively evil if we go ahead and perform the
act. Consequently, the person who is willing to act
with a doubtful conscience is ready to do evil, something which is forbidden by the moral law.

Solving the Doubt of Conscience

It follows from the second rule that one has to
solve the doubt before acting. This can be done in a
direct way, i.e., by further investigation and reflection.
If this does not result in solving the doubt, one can use
an indirect way and turn to the so-called *reflex principles*. These are general rules of prudence. They are
called reflex principles because we use them while reflecting on the state of doubt.

1. The first reflex principle concerns the morally
safer course.

The safer course means that alternative which

more certainly avoids evil and protects moral goodness. When we doubt whether the speed limit is 50 or 60 miles, it is safer to drive at 50 because this way we certainly avoid violating the law and avoid getting a ticket.

a. We are always allowed to choose the safer alternative and thus solve the practical doubt. This course, however, occasionally may be very costly and disadvantageous to us. For instance, if you doubt whether you have paid your taxes and you cannot directly investigate to get information before the deadline, to be on the safe side you can send a check to the Internal Revenue Service, but it is not necessary to do so. Nevertheless, there are cases when choosing the safer course is the only way of solving the practical doubt.

b. We are obliged to choose the safer course when we have the responsibility to obtain a certain goal and there is only one safe course to obtain it. A physician has to use a safer method and the safer medicine to save the life of a patient. A hunter must not shoot if he is in doubt about whether the moving object is an animal or a man. In criminal cases we "give the benefit of the doubt" to the accused to avoid the possible punishment of an innocent person.

2. The second reflex principle states that a *doubtful law does not bind*.

If we doubt

a. whether the law exists at all; or

b. whether the law applies to our case we are not bound to fulfill the doubtful obligation, because a duty cannot exist unless it is clearly seen to oblige us.

The reason upon which this reflex principle is based is the fact that a law has to be promulgated to reach the knowledge and will of an individual. Promulgation belongs to the essence of law because the moral law can realize its purpose only through the conscious and deliberate cooperation of a free being. Physical laws, on the other hand, obtain their goal by physical necessity and need not be known by the subject affected by these laws. The law of gravitation works without our knowledge and deliberate cooperation.

The Degree of Doubt

A doubt about the existence of a law can be supported by many arguments or just by a few. Hence, we can speak of different degrees of doubt and can ask what kind of arguments are required against the existence of an obligation to make it not binding.

Most moralists turn to the analysis of the nature of doubt and come to the conclusion that one solid argument against the existence of a law is sufficient to make it doubtful and not binding, even if there are other probable arguments for the existence of the law. The nature of doubt lies in the fact that there is a solid reason against the truth of a proposition that can induce a prudent and intelligent person to withhold his assent to it.

The technical term for this ethical stand is *probabilism*. It is derived from the basic contention of this theory that in order to be free from a duty it is sufficient that it be solidly probable that a law does not exist or does not apply to my case.

XIV
The Subjective Norm
of Morality

The judgment of conscience is the guide for the individual in making a moral decision. Hence, conscience can be called the subjective norm of morality. An act will be good or bad for a person according to the discernment of his intellect. Even in cases when a person follows the counsel of another man "against his better judgment," conscience draws the practical conclusion that it is morally good to accept the advice.

Conscience is called a subjective norm because an agent's judgment is influenced by his particular reasoning ability, by his intellectual insight, social background, prejudices he cannot overcome and other factors which color his judgment in such a way that it can deviate from the objective truth. The judgment of conscience is called the subjective norm of morality also in cases where it coincides with the objective truth, because it is a personal practical criterion for moral decisions.

This position may seem to open the door to the justification of subjective morality since nobody is entirely objective in all his judgments. Prejudices and our social and cultural environment play a rather important role in our decisions. Sigmund Freud called the judgments and prejudices imposed upon a person, the *superego*. It grows under the influence of parents and the social environment. This is not conscience in the strict sense of the term, because it is not a free personal judgment but an instinctive repetition of the opinion of others. Nevertheless, one cannot deny the influence on a person of the moral codes of a social class to which one belongs. Marx spoke about *bourgeois morality*. Today we use the terms, *middle class morality*, and *proletarian or communist morality*. These expressions indicate the influence of the moral codes of one's own social group. Biases and ideas at the board meeting of a large corporation differ from the biases of a trade union meeting. Furthermore, the historical setting also exerts a great influence on a person's moral outlook.[33] The moral standards of the Victorian age differed from the norms of post-war American society. All of us are children of our own age and are influenced by the taboos or permissiveness of our epoch.

Does this consideration, then, lead to moral relativism? It does not lead to the justification of moral relativism. It simply admits that the moral law is concretely applied by an individual whose judgment may deviate from objective truth, while the individual is obliged to follow the honest judgment of his intellect no matter in what age or milieu he lives. Hence concrete, practical morality is personal, and in some cases it inevitably becomes subjective and relative. On the other hand, it logically follows from our previous considerations that we are obliged to live according to objective truth in matters of morality and are bound to "form" our conscience in such a way that its judgments coincide with reality. The moral law does not condone bourgeois or proletarian morality but urges us to get rid of our prejudices and to judge the rightness or wrongness of actions objectively. The human intellect, however, is a finite means in our search for truth and a person can make errors in his judgment in spite of his best efforts.

It is important to remain intellectually open so that we will not be enclosed in our subjective evaluation of morality but give serious consideration to the opinion of others and be ready to change even an ingrained conviction when truth demands it. If a person surmises that he may be the victim of error, he has to reflect honestly on the problem and try to come to an objective judgment. It is not easy to break away from ingrained opinions, but the moral law demands this from us for the sake of truth. The moral law obliges us to uphold the ideal of the objectively correct moral judgment, to which we have to draw as near as we can.

XV
Freedom of Conscience

Always obey your certain conscience is the basic and most important law of individual morality. Since every duty has a corresponding right, it follows that the most fundamental individual right is freedom of conscience, i.e., our right to live and act according to our honest convictions. As we have seen earlier, civil societies are formed to defend the right of individuals and to promote the common good. We can conclude, then, that one of the weightiest duties of civil societies is the protection of freedom of conscience.

It is obvious, however, that the consciences of individuals may conflict with one another. Consequently, civil authorities are faced with the task of solving the conflicts of the consciences of their citizens. Are there any ethical principles that might guide us in solving these not infrequent collisions?

The general principle for the solution of these clashes is deduced from the nature and hierarchy of duties and rights. It could be expressed in the rule that the stronger and more certain rights prevail over the weaker and less certain ones. The application of this rule, however, may encounter numerous difficulties because it may not be easy to decide which one of the rights is stronger and consequently should have priority over the other. One way to determine the priority of a certain right is to investigate the harmful effects of the acts a person performs in obedience to his conscience. As long as the effects are confined to the agent, are relatively harmless, and the acts are not forced upon others, the agent's freedom of conscience must be protected. If a person is convinced that it is wrong to eat meat and concludes that he must be a vegetarian, he has the right to follow his conscience as long as he does not force his convictions on others. If somebody is of the opinion that even moderate drinking is wrong, he has the right to be a "teetotaler" but he does not have the right to force his conviction on others.

What happens if the acts commanded by one's conscience cause harm to the agent, as in the case of refusing medical treatment out of religious conviction? As long as the agent is mentally competent and does not force this conviction on others, for instance, on his children, he has the right to follow his conscience. A person in a terminal illness may follow his conscience and refuse the use of life-supporting devices. His right to do this is not granted to him by positive legislation but by the natural law. Civil authorities, on the other hand, have to enforce the right of children to medical treatment against the religious conviction of their parents because the right to life is basic and society must defend the rights of the incompetent.

Should civil authorities prevent suicides? Most nations have legislation in this regard based on the assumption that persons attempting suicide are not entirely competent and should be defended against the harmful effects of their ill-considered acts.

The problem becomes more difficult when people, alluding to their freedom of conscience, do things which harm the common good and the rights of others, as in the case of disseminating pornography or literature advocating violence and subversive actions. Citizens and their children evidently have the stronger right not to be exposed to obscenity against their will and not to be endangered by violent and subversive reading material. If subversive literature is not just a theoretical discussion of violence but a call to action imperiling public order, civil authorities have the duty to protect the citizens' rights to peace and an orderly life.

The conscience of a person may conflict with the laws of his country. Is a man obliged to obey the laws of his land in this case in order to avoid harming the public order? If the action commanded by a positive law is in contradiction with the natural law, one has to obey the natural law rather than the positive law. For instance, if a positive law prescribed the practice of a state religion or forbade the practice of religion at all, an individual would be obliged to follow his own conviction in this regard and go against the law of the state. Unfortunately, this case is not just theoretical speculation and a distant memory of past religious or political intolerance. Our own age is a witness to many limitations of freedom of religion and freedom of legitimate political activity. If a government were engaged in a war, or in the suppression of basic rights at home, and a man holds these as unethical, he should refuse cooperation in such activities even if it means imprisonment or some other kind of punishment. We must be willing to make sacrifices in leading a moral life, because the refusal to undergo hardship in the pursuit of moral values is an unethical decision, contradicting our commitment to morality.

Conclusion

If you have persevered up to this page, reading about and considering the principles of morality, you will most likely agree that ethics is not simply an abstract, academic study but that it is an extremely important part of the daily life of every individual and every community.

Notwithstanding the evident importance of morality, the mood at universities and colleges as well as outside the circles of higher education, occasionally turns against the study of moral values. We are told that the enormous problems of the modern world can only be solved by science, and that consequently it is important that students in higher education spend their time studying science, technology and the many skills that are necessary for the smooth operation of our complex society.

Nobody denies the importance and necessity of science and of the many skills without which the huge number of people of this planet could not reach even the animal level of existence. But one can become a "civilized" brute, that is, a person who uses the products of science to degrade or endanger human life. The creations of science are not morally good or bad, but they can be used for good or evil. Ethics takes over where science completes its work, and moral principles determine the right use of the fruits of science. Nuclear energy can be used for making atomic bombs,

139

killing millions of people and even blowing up the planet or it can be used for producing much-needed electric power. What we do with an invention is even more important than the invention itself.

It seems that presently we are experiencing a change of mood in educational circles concerning the importance of moral values. It has been discovered again that "value-free" education produces skilled persons who will have no scruples to use other human beings for their own selfish purposes, who will not hesitate to abuse political or economic power, giving only lip service to justice and the dignity of man. The recognition of moral values and the trend seriously to consider these values as a subject for academic study is a healthy development. Such a study may not lead to complete agreement on every detail of morality but we can establish at least a consensus about the most important moral principles without which human life would not be worth living.

The study of ethics, however, is not just an academic subject. The larger part of human life is enacted outside of schools. The important moral decisions affecting individuals and communities are made in the arena of everyday life. It is imperative for everybody to have clear ideas about moral values, but it is especially necessary for those who have power to affect the lives of others. Almost all political, economic or personal decisions involve moral values which greatly affect the humanity of our lives. Every morally wrong decision will influence others for the worse and every morally right decision for the better. Furthermore, the bad effects of an evil act boomerang on the agent who performs it. A person may engage in shoplifting to get some economic gain but ultimately he will pay higher prices for any merchandise he buys because the hidden costs of shoplifting will force prices higher. It has been reported that shoplifting costs the nation $5 billion a year. This means that the consumer, including the shoplifter, has to pay for pilferage, the cost of security to prevent shoplifting, and so on. Honesty is a moral value, and when it is lacking in people, human life becomes degraded and less fulfilled. Newspapers are filled every day with reports about crooked practices, corruption, rip-offs and forms of cheating which, in some way, affect all of us. Any evil act produces ripples that extend far beyond the place of impact.

Plato, in his *Republic*, favored a stable community that would not change in size or in its economic system. His idea of stability has never been achieved, for the world of man is dynamic and is in constant change, sometimes even fraught with violent explosions. The ethical principles that were discussed in this book can guide us through these incessant mutations and give us the necessary balance and assurance for leading a genuinely good human life. We have to learn to apply the unchanging principles to the changing world around us.

The majesty of the moral law calls us to solidarity with our fellowmen so that we make their lives more fruitful and worthwhile. If we are considerate of the well-being of others, our own lives become more meaningful, more "humanized," and we draw nearer our ultimate end, an end that beckons to us throughout our life and lends us the energy to go on amidst the trials, joys and hopes of our existence.

Selected Bibliography

Aquinas, St. Thomas. *Basic Writings*. 2 vols. Edited by A. C. Pegis. New York: Random House, 1945.

———. *Summa Contra Gentiles*. Translated as *On the Truth of the Catholic Faith*, by A. C. Pegis, J. F. Anderson, V. Bourke, C. J. O'Neil. Garden City, New York: Hanover House, 1955–1957.

———. *The Summa Theologica*. 22 vols. 2nd revised edition. Translated by the Fathers of the English Dominican Province. London: Burns Oates, 1912–1936. American Edition, New York: Benziger Brothers, 1947.

Aristotle. *Nichomachean Ethics*. Translated, with an introduction and notes, by Martin Ostwald. New York: The Library of Liberal Arts, 1962.

Ayer, Alfred Jules. *Language, Truth and Logic*. London: Victor Gollancz, Ltd., 1950.

Beauvoir, Simone de. *The Ethics of Ambiguity*. New York: Philosophical Library, 1948.

Bentham, Jeremy. *An Introduction to the Principles of Morals and Legislation*. New York: Russell & Russell, Inc., Publishers, 1962.

Bourke, Vernon J. *History of Ethics*. Garden City, New York: Doubleday and Co., 1968.

Butler, Joseph. *The Works of Joseph Butler*. Vol. 2. Oxford: The Clarendon Press, 1874.

Collins, James. *The Existentialists*. Chicago: Henry Regnery Co., 1952.

Comte, Auguste. *The Positive Philosophy of Auguste Comte*. 2 vols. Condensed by H. Martineau. London: Trubner & Co., 1853.

Cronin, Michael. *The Science of Ethics*. 2 vols. Revised Edition. Dublin: Gill and Son, 1939.

D'Arcy, Eric. *Conscience and its Right to Freedom*. New York: Sheed & Ward, 1961.

De George, Richard T. *Soviet Ethics and Morality*. Ann Arbor: The University of Michigan Press, 1969.

D'Entrèves, A. P. *Natural Law*. New York: Harper Torchbooks, 1965.

Edwards, Jonathan. *Freedom of the Will*. Edited by Arnold S. Kaufman and William K. Frankena. Indianapolis: The Bobbs-Merrill Co., Inc., 1969.

Engels, Friedrich. *Anti-Dühring; Herr Eugen Dühring's Revolution in Science*. Moscow: Foreign Languages Publishing House, 1962.

————. *Dialectics of Nature*. New York: International Publishers Co., Inc., 1960.

Ewing, A. C. *The Definition of Good*. New York: Macmillan, 1947.

————. *Ethics*. New York: The Free Press, 1953.

Fagothey, Austin, S.J. *Right and Reason*. 6th edition. Saint Louis: The C.V. Mosby Co., 1976.

Fletcher, Joseph. *Situation Ethics: The New Morality*. Philadelphia: The Westminster Press, 1966.

Flew, A. G. N. *Evolutionary Ethics*. New York: St. Martin's Press, 1967.

Frankena, William K. *Ethics*. 2nd Edition. Englewood Cliffs, N.J.: Prentice-Hall, Inc., 1973.

Gilson, Etienne. *Moral Values and Moral Life*. Hamden, Conn.: The Shoe String Press, Inc., 1961.

Hare, R. M. *Essays on Moral Concepts*. London: Macmillan Publishers, Ltd., 1972.

————. *The Language of Morals*. London: Oxford University Press, 1973.

Hobbes, Thomas. *Leviathan*. Edited by Michael Oakeshott. Oxford: 1947; New York: 1962.

Hudson, W. D. *Ethical Intuitionism*. New York: St. Martin's Press, 1967.

Hume, David. *Inquiry Concerning the Principles of Morals*. Indianapolis: The Bobbs-Merrill Co., Inc., 1957.

Hutcheson, Francis. *Illustrations on the Moral Sense*. Edited by Bernard Peach. Cambridge, Mass.: Belknap Press of Harvard University Press, 1971.

————. "An Inquiry into the Origin of Our Ideas of Beauty and Virtue." In *British Moralists*. Edited by

L.A. Selby-Bigge. Indianapolis: The Bobbs-Merrill Co., Inc., 1964.

Kant, Immanuel. *Critique of Practical Reason and other Writings in Moral Philosophy*. Translated and edited with an introduction by Lewis White Beck. Chicago: The University of Chicago Press, 1949.

_____. *Foundations of the Metaphysics of Morals*. Translated with an introduction by Lewis White Beck. New York: The Library of Liberal Arts, 1959.

_____. *Lectures on Ethics*. Translated by Louis Infield. New York: Harper Torchbooks, 1963.

Konstantinov, F. V., et al. *The Fundamentals of Marxist-Leninist Philosophy*. Moscow: Progress Publishers, 1974.

Kuusinen, O. V., et al. *Fundamentals of Marxism-Leninism*. Moscow: Foreign Languages Publishing House, 1963.

Lenin, Vladimir I. *Imperialism, the Highest Stage of Capitalism*. Moscow: Foreign Languages Publishing House, 1947.

_____. *The State and Revolution*. Moscow: Foreign Languages Publishing House, 1947; New York: International Publishers Co., Inc., 1954 (copyright 1932).

Lepp, Ignace. *The Authentic Morality*. New York: The Macmillan Co., 1965.

Macquarrie, John. *Three Issues in Ethics*. London: SCM Press, Ltd., 1970.

Maritain, Jacques. *Moral Philosophy: an Historical and Critical Survey of the Great Systems*. New York: Charles Scribner's Sons, 1964.

_____. *The Rights of Man and Natural Law*. Translated by Doris C. Anson. New York: Gordian Press, Inc., 1971.

Messner, Johannes. *Social Ethics*. St. Louis: B. Herder Book Co., 1949.

Mill, John Stuart. *Utilitarianism*. New York: The Library of Liberal Arts, 1957.

Moore, George Edward. *Ethics*. 2nd revised edition. New York: Oxford University Press, 1966.

_____. *Principia Ethica*. Cambridge: Cambridge University Press, 1959.

Nietzsche, Friedrich. "Thus Spoke Zarathustra," "Beyond

Good and Evil," "Genealogy of Morals." *In Collected Works*. New York: Russell & Russell Inc., Publishers, 1964.

O'Connor, D. J. *Free Will*. New York: Doubleday Publishing Co., 1971.

Ramsey, Paul. *Deeds and Rules in Christian Ethics*. New York: Charles Scribner's Sons, 1967.

Rand, Ayn, and Branden, Nathaniel. *The Virtue of Selfishness*. New York: The New American Library, Inc., 1964.

Rand, Benjamin, ed. *The Classical Moralists*. Boston: Houghton Mifflin Co., 1909.

Raphael, D. D., ed. *British Moralists*. 2 vols. Oxford: The Clarendon Press, 1969.

Rommen, Heinrich. *The Natural Law*. St. Louis: B. Herder Book Co., 1948.

Ross, W. D. *Foundations of Ethics*. Oxford: The Clarendon Press, 1939.

Rousseau, Jean Jacques. *The Social Contract*, New York: Hafner Publishing Co., Inc., 1947.

Selby-Bigge, L. A. *British Moralists*. Indianapolis: The Bobbs-Merrill Co., Inc., 1964.

Shaftesbury, Earl of. *Characteristics of Men, Manners, Opinions and Times*. Edited by John M. Robertson. London: 1900.

Simon, Yves R. *Freedom of Choice*. Edited by Peter Wolff. New York: Fordham University Press, 1969.

_____. *The Tradition of Natural Law*. New York: Fordham University Press, 1965.

Smith, Adam. *The Theory of Moral Sentiments*. New Rochelle, N.Y.: Arlington House, Inc., 1969.

Stevenson, Charles L. *Ethics and Language*. New Haven: Yale University Press, 1960.

_____. *Facts and Values: Studies in Ethical Analysis*. New Haven: Yale University Press, 1963.

Stroll, A. *The Emotive Theory of Ethics*. Berkeley, California: University of California Press, 1954.

Taylor, Richard. *Good and Evil: a New Direction*. New York: The Macmillan Co., 1970.

Thielicke, Helmut. *Theological Ethics #1*. London: Adam & Charles Black, 1968.

Tucker, Robert. *Philosophy and Myth in Karl Marx*. 2nd edition. Cambridge: Cambridge University Press, 1972.

Warnock, Mary. *Ethics Since 1900*. 2nd revised edition. London: Oxford University Press, 1966.

Wetter, Gustav A. *Dialectical Materialism*. New York: Praeger, 1958.

————. *Soviet Ideology Today*. London: Heinemann, 1966.

Wild, John. *Plato's Modern Enemies and the Theory of Natural Law*. Chicago: The University cf Chicago Press, 1953.

Notes

Chapter V

1. For a brief discussion of freedom, cf. J. F. Donceal, S.J., *Philosophical Anthropology*, (New York: Sheed and Ward, 1967), pp. 365–406.

2. B. F. Skinner, *Beyond Freedom and Dignity*, (New York: Knopf, 1971), p. 189.

Chapter VII

1. A. J. Ayer, *Language, Truth and Logic*, (London: Victor Gollancz, Ltd., 1950).

2. C. L. Stevenson, *Ethics and Language*, (New Haven: Yale University Press, 1946).

3. G. E. Moore, *Principia Ethica*, (London: Cambridge University Press, 1903).

4. G. E. Moore, *Ethics*, 2nd rev. ed., (New York: Oxford University Press, 1966).

5. Shaftesbury, *An Inquiry Concerning Virtue and Merit*, (London: 1699); *The Moralists, or Philosophical Rhapsody*, (London: 1709).

6. Joseph Butler, *Fifteen Sermons*, ed. by W.R. Metthews, (London: Oxford University Press, 1949); *Works*, ed. W.E. Gladstone, (London: Oxford University Press, 1910).

7. Francis Hutcheson, *Inquiry into the Original of Our Ideas of Beauty and Virtue*, (London: 1725).

8. Adam Smith, *Theory of Moral Sentiments*, (Edinburgh: 1759).

8a. For a good summary of the two types of utilitarianism, see William K. Frankena, *Ethics*. 2nd ed. (Englewood Cliffs: Prentice-Hall, 1973), pp. 34-43.

9. J. S. Mill, *Dissertations and Discussions*, 5 vols., (Boston: 1865–75), I., p. 358.

10. Aristotle, *Nichomachean Ethics*, Bk. 3, Ch. 6–12, Bks. 4–6.

11. Cf. F. V. Konstantinov et al., *The Fundamentals of Marxist-Leninist Philosophy*, (Moscow: Progress Publishers, 1974).

12. For a detailed analysis of Marxist ethics cf. Richard T. De George, *Soviet Ethics and Morality*, (Ann Arbor: The University of Michigan Press, 1969).

13. O. V. Kuusinen et al., *Fundamentals of Marxism-Leninism*, (Moscow: Foreign Languages Publishing House, 1963), p. 35.

14. Cf. Konstantinov, *op. cit.*, pp. 130–152.

15. Ibid., p. 336.

16. Ibid.

17. Cf. Gustav A. Wetter, *Dialectical Materialism*, (New York: Praeger, 1958); *Soviet Ideology Today*, (London: Heinemann, 1966).

18. Joseph Fletcher, *Situation Ethics: The New Morality*, (Philadelphia: The Westminster Press, 1966), p. 26.

19. *Ibid.*, p. 79.

Chapter VIII

20. Ignace Lepp, *The Authentic Morality*, (New York: The Macmillan Co., 1968), p. 51.

21. John Macquarrie, *Three Issues in Ethics*, (London: SCM Press, 1970), p. 52.

Chapter IX

22. Cf. Cornelius J. van der Poel, "The Principle of Double Effect," in Charles E. Curran, ed., *Absolutes in Moral Theology?*, (Washington: Corpus Books, 1968).

Chapter X

23. For a detailed history of the natural law see: Heinrich A. Rommen, *The Natural Law*, (St. Louis: B. Herder, 1947).

24. Quoted in Heinrich A. Rommen, *The State in Catholic Thought*, (St. Louis: B. Herder, 1947), p. 156.

25. *Laws*, I, XVI, translated by C. W. Keyes, in The Loeb Classical Library. Quoted in Rommen, *The Natural Law*, (St. Louis: B. Herder, 1947), p. 24.

26. Cf. Helmut Thielecke, *Theological Ethics I*, (London: Adam & Charles Black, 1968), p. 385.

27. Quoted in Thielecke, *op. cit.*, p. 386.

28. *New York Times*, March 18, 1977, p. A10.

Chapter XI

29. Cf. St. Thomas Aquinas, *Summa theologica*, I.a, II.ae, q.97.a1.

Chapter XII

30. Cf. J. Messner, *Social Ethics*, (St. Louis: B. Herder, 1949), pp. 148–154.

31. *Ibid.*, pp. 153–54.

32. *Ibid.*, p. 152.

Chapter XIV

33. Cf. John Macquarrie, *Three Issues in Ethics*, (London: SCM Press, 1970), p. 114.

Index